The Neglected Firm

The Neglected Firm

Every manager must manage two firms:
the present one and the future one

Jorge A. Vasconcellos e Sá

with the collaboration of

Tito Xavier and Pedro Leitão

palgrave

Published 2002 by
PALGRAVE
Houndmills, Basingstoke, Hampshire RG21 6XS and
175 Fifth Avenue, New York, N.Y. 10010
Companies and representatives throughout the world

PALGRAVE is the new global academic imprint of
St. Martin's Press LLC Scholarly and Reference Division and
Palgrave Publishers Ltd (formerly Macmillan Press Ltd).

ISBN 0–333–98712–8 hardcover

This book is printed on paper suitable for recycling and made from fully managed and sustained forest sources.

A catalogue record for this book is available from the British Library.

Library of Congress Cataloging-in-Publication Data

Sá, Jorge Alberto Sousa de Vasconcellos e.
The neglected firm : every manager must manage two firms : the present one and the future one / Jorge A. Vasconcellos e Sá.
p. cm.
Includes bibliographical references and index.
ISBN 0–333–98712–8
1. Strategic planning. 2. Industrial management. I. Title.

HD30.28 .S2 2002
658.4'012—dc21 2001060295

Editing and origination by
Aardvark Editorial, Mendham, Suffolk

10 9 8 7 6 5 4 3 2 1
11 10 09 08 07 06 05 04 03 02

Printed and bound in Great Britain by
Creative Print & Design (Wales), Ebbw Vale

To my family

Contents

List of Figures

List of Figures

List of Tables

CHAPTER 1

Introduction: The Neglected Firm (every manager must manage two firms)

Every manager must manage two companies at the same time: the present one and the future one – the former through the functional departments (marketing, finance, and so on), the latter through the most recent management area: planning (see Figure 1.1). This is the area about which least is known, the one that constitutes both a risk and a great opportunity. Let's analyse this problem in further detail.

Any book of strategy indicates that the success of a company depends on it being, at one and the same time, effective and efficient (see Figure 1.2), that is, doing the right things right – operating in attractive market areas and providing low costs.[1,2,3] Therefore, the first major task of a manager is to manage this effectiveness/efficiency on a day-to-day basis, that is, to manage the present company. This means two things:

1. In terms of effectiveness (to do the right things), ensuring that the strategic plan is properly implemented, which means that:
   - the *products/services* have the characteristics demanded by the target segments;
   - the promotion is centred on what constitutes value for the customer (fulfilment of the customer's *needs*);

- the marketing focus is effectively directed at the target *customers*; and
- penetration of the *geographic areas* takes place in accordance with the plan.

Therefore, product/service, need, customer, and geographic area are the four variables that define the strategy of a company: the four sides of the strategic square within which its business is carried on. Any firm can have one or more strategic squares which define their business(es).

2. Within the field of the day-to-day, or urgent tasks, there are all the other tasks linked to efficiency (to do things right): negotiating with suppliers, reviewing the latest cost accounting report, settling a particular financial matter, dealing with an advertising agency, selecting a candidate, phoning a customer, managing the political aspects of the industry (lobbying for beneficial laws, dealing with regulatory agencies and so on). That is, dozens of small tasks that occupy the day-to-day life of the manager. It is for this reason that it is said that management is a set of interruptions constantly interrupted by interruptions: a paper to send here, a phone call there, a meeting somewhere else.

   Both management of present effectiveness and efficiency are in the hands of the office of the chairman and the functional departments of a company (marketing, manufacturing, finance, accounting, human resources, information systems and administration (hygiene, catering, maintenance of installations, security and communications – both internal and external) (Figure 1.1).

Therefore managing the present effectiveness and efficiency is one aspect of the management of the company of the present. It involves:

- attaining effectiveness through implementation of present strategy
- ensuring efficiency through dozens of small, day-to-day tasks (Figure 1.2).[1,2,3]

Figure 1.1 The standard organization chart

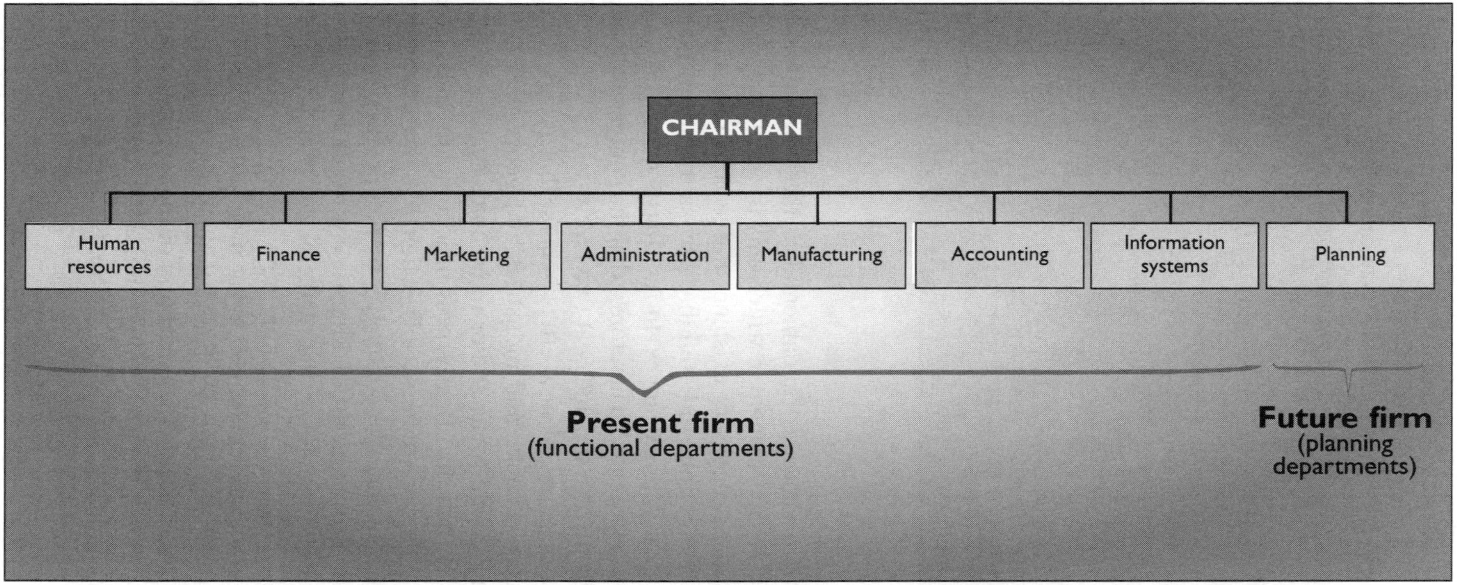

Figure 1.2 The traditional way of seeing a company optimization

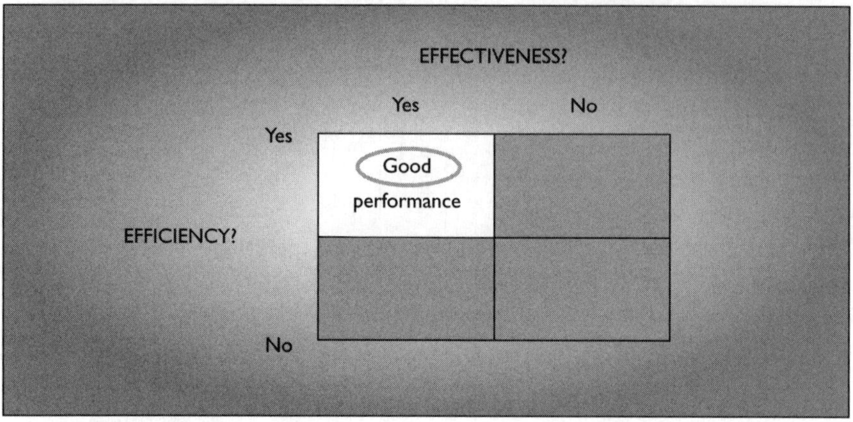

Good performance is fundamental to the survival of the company in a competitive environment in which only the strong survive. And, as Darwin said, 'in the struggle for existence not to be strong is almost to be guilty'. But, as Heraclitus and Buddha also said, the only constant in life is change. Everything changes. In A. Allais's words: 'History's waste basket is full of long trends'. Therefore, what the company should be in the future differs from what it is today at two levels.

First, in terms of new effectiveness, that is, of reanalysing the products, needs, clients, and industries and geographic areas on which the company should focus and/or move into. Perhaps, but one must rethink the matter, and the effectiveness of a company must constantly be reappraised. The products, needs, clients and geographical areas which together constitute the company's market position must be reanalysed.

Second, in terms of seeking new ways of being efficient, whether or not strategy (position in the marketplace) changes. Would it be better to merge two departments that are now separated into a division in order to profit from scale economies? What if an activity now carried on in-house were farmed out? Doesn't that section need to be reorganized?

All this concerns the possibility of the company doing different things in the future, or the same things in a different way, that is, thinking about the (our) company of the future. So, the second aspect of management is that, in addition to managing the company of the present, a manager also has to manage the company of the future.

However, if he manages just the former and not the second, given change, his company will soon become obsolete. If he manages just the latter and neglects the former, it will never reach the future. Consequently, the competitiveness of a company depends on proper management of the short term (the present company) and the introduction of qualitative jumps (managing the future company). Corporate survival requires both managerial and entrepreneurial skills, the former to manage the present firm and the latter to create the future one. A CEO must, therefore, be both a manager and an entrepreneur.

This is the eternal dilemma of management, the reconciliation of the urgent (day-to-day) and the important (the future). In order to deal with the urgent the chairman has his office and the functional departments. But who deals with the important matter, the future of the company, and how to do it?

Managing the company of the future

In some companies this is done on a nonsystematic basis, in bursts or on impulse. This is known as MEAI (Management by Erratic and Aleatory Impulses). 'Colleagues, the boss has had an idea: what if we bought company X?' 'Lads, the boss had lunch with the chairman of company Y: what if we move into geographic zone Z?' 'May I have your attention please: the boss is fed up with Thomas. He wants us to get over there to study his department and reorganize it from top to bottom.'

In such a situation, the company of the present is managed well or not so well by the functional departments. But the company of the future is badly handled, in fits and starts. It is managed episodically, in bits and pieces, with two serious negative implications. First, there is no guarantee that a given initiative is the best one, since it is analysed in isolation and not compared to others. Second, there's no idea about the compatibility of the various initiatives, because there's no global plan.

At heart, it is as though, for example, there was no overall marketing plan in the marketing department to which every initiative is subordinated. Thus, one would advertise one day on television programme X, decide to sponsor event Z on another day, implement a merchandising programme

Table 1.1 Reasons why a planning department is needed to manage the future firm

1	To possess a whole, global plan of what one is trying to achieve, therefore guaranteeing mutual compatibility among the several actions
2	To have mental readiness
3	To obtain the right information
4	To ascertain adequate participation
5	To guarantee that decisions are taken sequentially in a rational way

on a third and so on, without ever taking into account whether the objective (customer) is common and whether, in comparison with other activities, they are the best measures, which requires that alternatives be drawn up. That is the reason for drawing up an overall marketing plan. That is also why we need a sequential, step-by-step approach to managing the future firm, otherwise it will be neglected. Besides these two, there are three other reasons which follow from them.

To manage the future firm within the small breaks that managing the present firm allows requires one's mind to jump from concrete, urgent problems, which require immediate action during a small time span, to more abstract, fundamental issues whose analysis requires large amounts of patience and time. This is not easily accomplished. Managing both the urgent and the important at the same time is difficult. Therefore a planning department is required.

However, even if one could easily make those jumps from the urgent to the important, one would still lack the information required for sound decisions: what are the growth rates in the various market segments? What are our competitors' strengths and weaknesses? What are the market's key success factors? And so on.

Finally, decisions regarding the future firm are so important that no one person should tackle them in isolation. The firm's chairman should at least listen to and debate them with his closest managers, which requires meetings. These need to be planned in advance, provided beforehand with due information, attended by the right audience and all organized in proper sequence.

In short, there are five reasons why the future firm must be managed in a formal, structured way. It is for these reasons that a planning department must exist to deal with the time dimension, with the company's future (see Table 1.1).

The functions of the planning department

The function of the planning department is twofold: to help top management think of new means of being effective (positioning in the marketplace) and new means of being efficient. That is, everything that is new. Not in bursts, in random, erratic impulses, but on an ongoing basis subject to an overall plan.

Therefore the planning department acts as a sort of chairman's war-room or general staff. Its role is to help the chairman (alone, or with his top management) to manage the company of the future.

To *help*, not to do! The person who decides is the one at the head of the troops, but for this he needs help. What sort of help? The planning department has six functions:

1. To take part in several meetings chaired by the chairman with line managers. Those meetings begin by rethinking current strategy (should some segments be scrapped? should a move be made into new ones? if so, which and why?) and end with the preparation of the company's budget. Along the way, there is the drawing up of the new strategic plan, the definition of the strategic business units (SBUs) within the company, the objectives of each SBU (market share and so on), the organization chart of each business area and so on. All these steps are explained in Chapters 3 to 9.

   The logic of this process must be perfectly dominated by the planning manager, and everything is decided at meetings that usually take place over three months, starting, for example, in September and ending in November with the definition of the budget for the following year.

   Taking part in meetings means not taking decisions but providing clarification about the documents, providing opinions if requested and accompanying the entire process. The planning manager is both the mechanic and navigator. He is not the pilot, the pilot is the chairman.

2. To define with the chairman and in respect of these meetings: their number; their date; the participants; and the location. This is known as the planning manual.

3. To supply the meetings with the required information. That is, to provide the necessary information to the chairman and top management, in the form of documents to be read before the meetings, so that decisions can be taken at the meeting. It's important to bear in mind that it is the chairman and senior management who take the decisions, not the planning manager. He attends the meetings just to clear up points connected with the documents.

   These documents comprise the industry segmentation matrix, the position of the competition, the growth forecasts for the various segments, the firm's strong and weak points compared to the competition, the potential opportunities detected by the customer analysis system (unsatisfied customer needs) and so on (see Figure 10.1).

4. To manage the information gathering system (client analysis system, for example), which has two objectives. First, to provide each planning meeting with the information needed for decisions to be taken. Second, to ensure that, outside the scope of the meetings, the required information about the market, the competition and so on is all centralized, simply structured and easily retrieved at the touch of a button.

5. To receive the plans that have been drawn up and integrate them in a systematic, simple, succinct manner that is easily consulted. These are mainly the company's strategic plan, the company's organization chart, the objectives of each SBU and the company's budget.

6. Lastly, throughout the year the planning department will study several alternatives to improve the working of the various sections (their efficiency level), either because they are key departments that handle critical success factors, or because their performance is below an acceptable minimum and consequently causes bottlenecks that threaten to disrupt the efficient working of the company. Some of this work can be identified at the beginning of the year and is therefore

included in a plan (to increase efficiency), and some is undertaken in the light of the needs that arise during the year.

Through these six activities (summarized in Table 1.2), the planning department will make sure that the firm changes both in terms of optimizing its effectiveness (market positioning, that is, its strategy) and efficiency: new and better ways of doing things, a new organization chart, new control mechanisms and so on. This pertains to the business administration area called planning.

So the future firm is achieved by changing either what will be done or how it will be done. All that is new. The present firm, in contrast, is a consequence of the day-to-day management by the chairman's office and the functional departments. The future competitiveness of a company depends on good management of the short term (the present company) and on introducing qualitative jumps (managing the future company).

In other words, any corporate executive must be both a manager (to deal with the present firm) and simultaneously an entrepreneur (to create the future one). Both – not either, or.

This is the eternal dilemma of management: the urgent (day-to-day) and the important (the future) have to be reconciled. Because, only when both firms (the present and future) are well managed is good performance achieved.

Table 1.2 The six functions of the planning department (and its manager)

1	To *take part* in the planning meetings (with line managers)
2	To define the numbers, date, participants and location of those meetings. This is known as the *planning manual*
3	To supply the meetings with the required *information*
4	To *manage* the company's information gathering process (client analysis system and so on)
5	To *integrate* all departmental plans into a single corporate plan
6	To improve the critical departments *efficiency* level

To manage the future firm is to manage the firm's time dimension; to manage the present firm is to optimize its status quo. Both are necessary, neither one alone is sufficient, if the organization is to survive. Thus, to the traditional way of looking at management, described in Figure 1.3.1 and corresponding to cell 1 in Figure 1.3.2, we must add cells 2, 3 and 4 of Figure 1.3.2 and thus achieve a modern way of looking at management.

This modern way demands that the tasks of all the cells in Figure 1.3.2, be done satisfactorily:

- the old tasks in the old ways (cell 1);
- the old tasks in a different (new) way (cell 2);
- the new tasks in the old way (done in the same way) (cell 3);
- the new tasks in a new way (cell 4).

Three noteworthy aspects

It would be helpful at this point to bear three aspects in mind:

- First, the existence of the strategy rethinking process does not mean that new opportunities will not be analysed if they arise. The advantage is that they will be analysed in the light of earlier reflection on the company's strengths, the market areas with greater growth potential and so on and their compatibility with other initiatives (synergy).
- Second, the work of the planning department – just as any other work – may all be done in-house or partially farmed out. What is essential is quality: to know precisely how to set up the sequential system of decisions, rather than fumbling about.
- Third, much of this is mumbo-jumbo for many companies, even for those with a planning department. With only a vague idea of what planning is, it is hard to set up the system. In the words of Seneca, 'there are no fair winds when you don't know which harbour to head for'. Those who sail have a similar saying: when you don't know where you want to go the wind always blows from the wrong direction.

Figure 1.3.1 Traditional way of looking at management (the 'present firm')

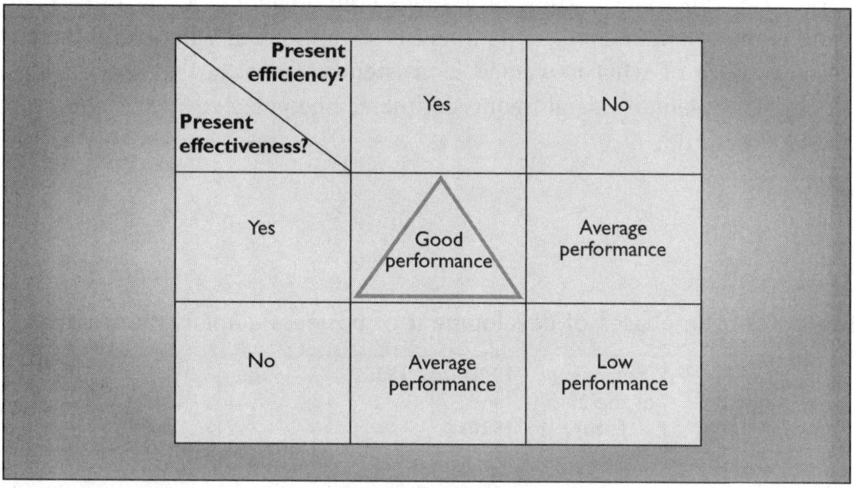

Figure 1.3.2 Modern way of looking at management

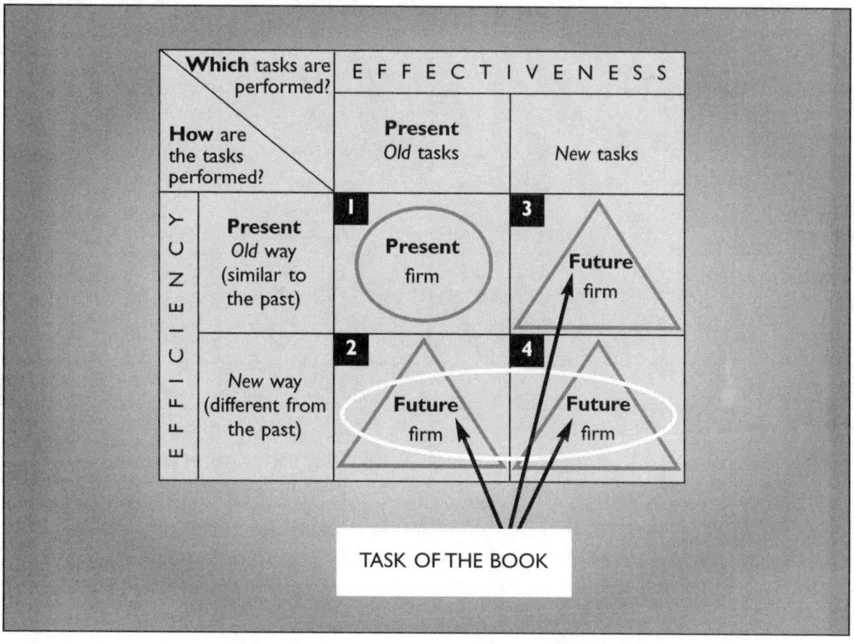

In many companies therefore, the fundamental role of the planning manager is to take along the water melon for the company picnic and little more. He sometimes carries out a few studies. There is an idea that planning is important and so a department is set up to deal with it. But there is no clear idea of what is wanted, consistently, from start to finish and in detail. The planning department sits there, unconnected in the company, doing very little.

Table 1.3 The phases of development of business administration areas

Areas \ Dates	Beginning of the 20th century	1900s and 1920s	1930s	1950s	1960s	1970s
Accounting (namely cost accounting)	✓					
Production management		✓				
Administrative areas (building maintenance, catering, hygiene, security, internal and external communications and so on)		✓				
Human resource management			✓			
Information system management				✓		
Finance				✓		
Marketing					✓	
Planning (specially strategic)*						✓

*Note: Although some books date back to the 1960s (Ansoff, Ackoff, and so on) and even to the 1950s with the business policy texts first introduced by Learned, Christensen and so on at Harvard, it was the 1970s that saw the start of the boom in this discipline

The reason is simple: planning, especially strategic planning, is management's most recent area of development, dating from the late 1970s, compared to others that appeared far earlier: management accounting (major developments of cost accounting at the beginning of the century – although the system of double entry for general accounting was developed much earlier by Luca Paccioli), production management (1930s and 40s); human resources management (1930s) and so on (see Table 1.3). Therefore, it is not surprising that less is known about planning, in companies, universities and consultancy firms, and so only by chance will it be achieved.

But the basic question remains: how can you be a good general strategist without an adequate general staff (planning department)?

Conclusion: planning, a risk that is a great opportunity

There are two types of ignorance, unconscious and conscious. The unconscious is the worst; you don't know what you don't know; whereas, in the latter, at least you know what you don't know. In planning, many are unconsciously ignorant, a few consciously so, and still fewer are knowledgeable. Therefore, investment in planning constitutes a risk,[2] but also a great opportunity![3]

An opportunity – first, because at the present stage those who implement this management area well will have taken a step forward and gained competitive advantage more easily than in other areas (marketing, finance and so on) in which knowledge is far more widespread.

Second, since every manager must manage two companies (the present one and the future one), he must, in order to gain competitive advantage in the former, manage seven departments better. However, to gain advantage in the latter, it is sufficient to be better only in the planning department (see Figure 1.1). Thus, this is the area in which the great management opportunity of the present resides (see Figure 1.4).

This book explains how to exploit such an opportunity. Chapter 2 presents an overview of the step-by-step approach to how to do it. Chapters 3 to 9 discuss each step in some detail and Chapter 10 presents the planning department's internal organization necessary to implement the steps from Chapters 3 to 9.

Figure 1.4 The role of the planning and functional departments in managing the two firms

Managing the company of the / through the	Future (the new)	Present (the current)
Planning department	✓	
Functional departments (production, finance, marketing and so on)		✓

Some of the material (techniques, theories and concepts) is new. Some is borrowed from other authors, whose contribution is highly important. Whatever the case, all the material is organized in a new way in order to provide a simple, sequential, step-by-step approach to manage the future firm.

CHAPTER 2

A Step-by-step Approach to Managing the Neglected Firm

Management of the future firm requires seven main steps:

1. Define the present strategy of the firm (Chapter 3)
2. Evaluate the present strategy (Chapter 4)
3. Create alternatives (Chapter 5)
4. Select the best of those alternatives (Chapter 6)
5. Synthesize steps 2–4 in a new strategy (Chapter 7)
6. Implement that new strategy (Chapter 8)
7. Change critical departments in search of new efficiency (Chapter 9).

In the following chapters each step will be analysed in some detail (a summary of all seven steps may be found in Figure 2.2). Let us now, however, provide an overview of the whole process.

Step 1: Define the present strategy of the firm

Before anything else, one must have a clear idea of the present market position of the firm, what its strategy is, and where it is invoicing and where its clients are. Thus, information regarding this year's clients' invoices needs to be obtained from the accounting system in order to determine the type of clients (and the proportion), that is, their industries, segments and geographical areas.

Therefore the starting point is a concrete, thorough knowledge of the market segments that the firm is in, because it is these which cover the firm's present costs, and where the company has experience. Strong reasons are required to exchange the old (certain) for the new (uncertain).

Step 2: Evaluate the present strategy

The purpose of evaluating the present strategy is to see if one should maintain a presence in all market segments or pull out of some (see Chapter 4). And, if the latter is true, which?

To this end, all the market segments in which the firm currently operates should be placed in a matrix, as shown in Figure 2.1.[4,11] The matrix examines the current market segments from two angles: their attractiveness (in terms of sales volume, margin and rate of growth) and the strength of the firm's competitive position within them.[11]

The purpose of the exercise is to determine which segments are both unattractive and uncompetitive for the firm. They will then fall in the boot-like area of the matrix (lower right corner) and thus should be rejected (see Figure 2.1).

Naturally enough, one, two or more segments may fall within the rejection zone depending on how conditions have changed since the present strategic plan was drawn up: changes in the rates of market growth, the entry of new (and stronger) competitors, technological changes implying new success factors and so on.

Because only change is constant, today's evaluation will almost certainly differ from that carried out one or two years previously when the last strategic plan was made. As a result, the firm should prepare to abandon the segments which now fall within the rejection zone.

The examination matrix will provide an indication of the degree of concentration a firm should adopt – higher, lower or zero – that is, the level of its focus,[36] in terms of current activities. But what about other activities in which the firm is not presently engaged? Should it adopt them or not? And if so, which?

Figure 2.1 The examination matrix

Source: Adapted from Aaker, D., *Strategic Market Management*, 4th edn, 1998

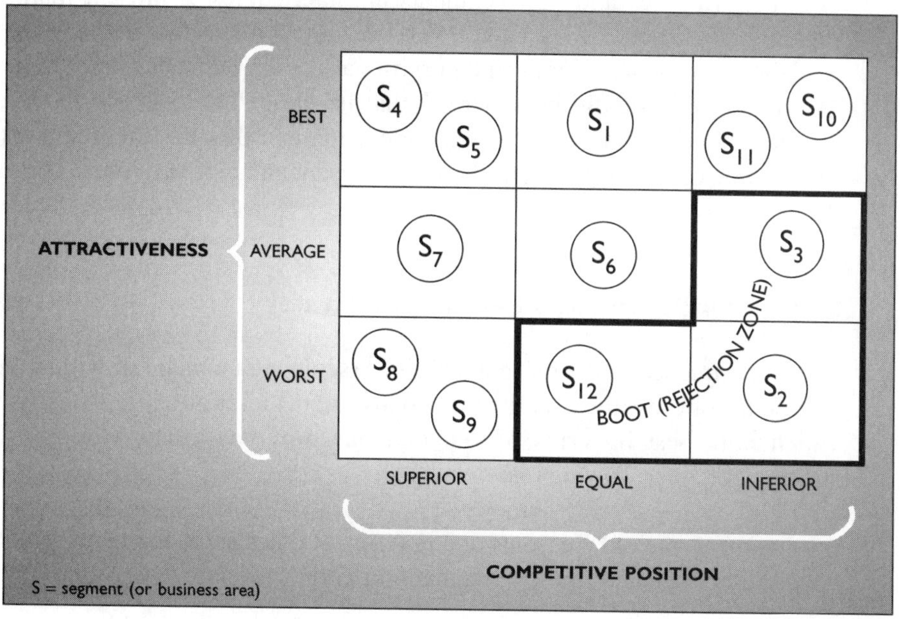

Step 3: Create alternatives

To decide on such a matter, one must first of all create strategic alternatives (see Chapter 5).[36,5,6] Strategic alternatives can be innovations (totally new activities that no other firm undertakes) or simply industry segments in which the firm does not currently operate but others do.

Innovations are suggested by the client analysis system which periodically collects information on questions such as: which client needs are not presently satisfied? What is value for the customer? Which type of clients are not presently targeted?

Simple opportunities in terms of segments come from segmenting each industry the firm is in and then considering as entry opportunities those segments which are closer to present operations in particular.

Step 4: Select the best of those alternatives

Both opportunities and new segments are alternatives to present market standing. But should they be followed or not? This is the decision that needs to be made, and for such a purpose, a selection criteria is required.

This criteria should be synergy,[6] that is, the extent to which there is resource sharing (sales force, machinery, plants, distribution channels, administrative space and so on) between present and new activities. This is the subject of Chapter 6.

Step 5: Synthesize steps 2–4 in a new strategy

As a consequence of the present activities (segments) which fall within the rejection zone of the examination matrix and the strategic alternatives which rank best in terms of synergy, one now has a new (proposed) strategy (Chapter 7) which is:

- *similar* to the old (present) one in terms of old market segments which were not rejected in the examination matrix of Figure 2.1
- *different* from the old (present) strategy in terms of: old (present) market segments rejected since they fell within the boot of the examination matrix; and *new activities*, generated either by the client analysis system or by segmentation, which are highly synergetic with present ones.

Step 6: Implement that new strategy

Here there are three vectors that need to be taken into account (Chapter 8). The first has to do with structure. The second concerns processes: the objectives of SBUs, the programmes to achieve them and the budget to control the programmes. The third vector is related to functional plans: marketing, finance (budgets), production, personnel (human resources planning) and so on. (That is the subject of specialized books on marketing, finance, production and so on. This book will concentrate solely on organizational (structure) and procedural (long range and so on) planning.)

Figure 2.2 A step-by-step approach to managing the future firm

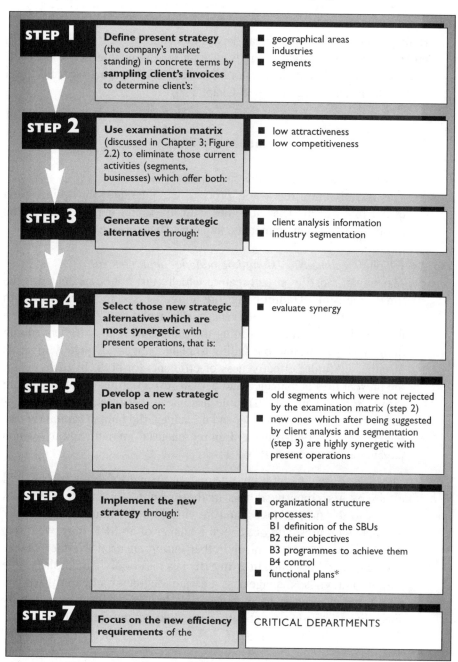

STEP 1	**Define present strategy** (the company's market standing) in concrete terms by **sampling client's invoices** to determine client's:	■ geographical areas ■ industries ■ segments
STEP 2	**Use examination matrix** (discussed in Chapter 3; Figure 2.2) to eliminate those current activities (segments, businesses) which offer both:	■ low attractiveness ■ low competitiveness
STEP 3	**Generate new strategic alternatives** through:	■ client analysis information ■ industry segmentation
STEP 4	**Select those new strategic alternatives which are most synergetic** with present operations, that is:	■ evaluate synergy
STEP 5	**Develop a new strategic plan** based on:	■ old segments which were not rejected by the examination matrix (step 2) ■ new ones which after being suggested by client analysis and segmentation (step 3) are highly synergetic with present operations
STEP 6	**Implement the new strategy** through:	■ organizational structure ■ processes: B1 definition of the SBUs B2 their objectives B3 programmes to achieve them B4 control ■ functional plans*
STEP 7	**Focus on the new efficiency requirements** of the	CRITICAL DEPARTMENTS

Note: *That is the subject of specialized books on marketing, finance, production, etc. This book will concentrate solely on organizational (structure) and processes (B1 (SBUS); B2 (objectives); B3 (programme); and B4 (control)

Step 7: Change critical departments in search of new efficiency

Here the focus is on the critical departments and bottlenecks in search of higher levels of efficiency. There is an analysis of how internal tasks can be rendered more efficient, with even higher levels of productivity and lower costs (which will be addressed in Chapter 9).

Summary of some key points in the 7-step process

1. *What will guarantee a firm's success?*
   The overall aim of this whole process is to guarantee the optimization of the future firm. That, together with the sound management of the present firm, will guarantee a company's success (see Figure 2.3).[7]

2. *Which new dimension should be added to management?*
   The single, most important feature which must not be neglected is the time dimension. Traditionally, literature stressed the pursuit of both present efficiency and effectiveness. But that is not enough. Indeed, a firm can be both effective (doing the right things) and efficient (doing things right) at present but failing to plan changes adequately in terms of either its future effectiveness or efficiency or both. In such a case, the present firm is managed and perhaps even optimized but the future firm is sorely neglected. Trouble lies ahead, because short- and long-term competitiveness both depend on managerial human capital (whose focus is the *present* firm) and entrepreneurial human capital[6] (which targets the *future* firm) (Box 2.1).

   The overall result of failing adequately to manage both aspects will either be a serious weakness in the present or a problem when it comes to the firm adapting and moving into the future. That is why any manager, president or general manager of an SBU must wear two hats – one managerial and the other entrepreneurial. Neither can be neglected and both must fit. (An SBU is a part or division of the whole corporation whose manager has a certain degree of autonomy and can be evaluated by a profit or investment budget. If the firm is totally specialized in products, clients, needs served and geographical area, then it is equivalent to an SBU.)

Figure 2.3 Company optimization requires sound management of both the present and the future firm

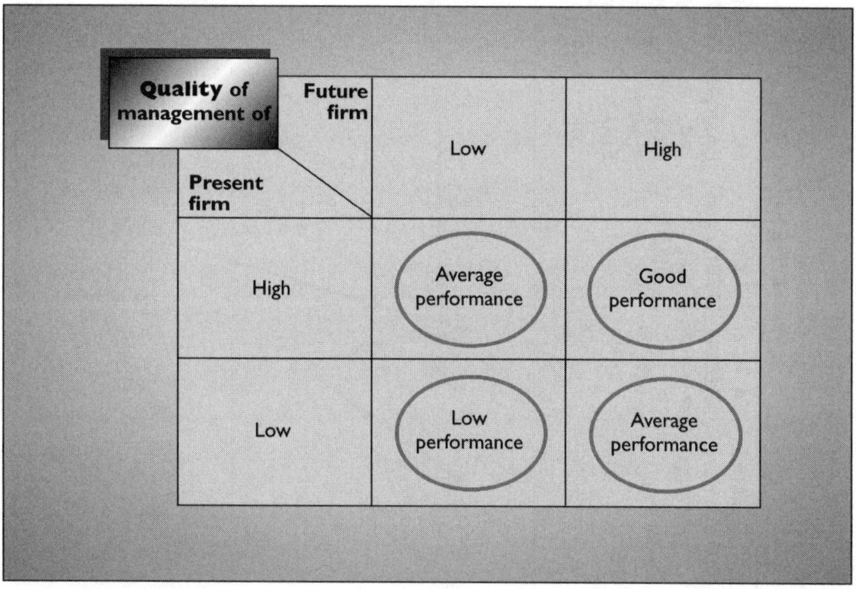

BOX 2.1

Another way of looking at the relationship between the present and future firm is by realizing that there are four necessary conditions for a firm's performance to be optimized:

1. Good present effectiveness

   Plus

2. Good present efficiency

   Plus

3. Good future effectiveness

   Plus

4. Good future efficiency

The more a firm fails in one or more of these areas, the more it will be under-performing.

Table 2.1 Front page of the planning manual

Decisions / Participants	1	2	3	4	5	6 Implementation			
	Definition of present strategy	**Evaluation of present strategy**	**Generation of the strategic alternative (output of client analysis and industry segmentation)**	**Evaluation of the strategic alternatives (through synergy)**	**Definition of a new strategy**	**6A Overall structure**	**6B SBUs and their objectives**	**6C Programmes and structure of each SBU**	**6D Budget and other control mechanisms**
President									
First management level									
Second management level									
Third management level									
Fourth management level									

3. *Who helps the president in managing the present and future in the firm?*
   The president is helped in managing the present firm by the functional departments and he is helped in managing the future firm by the planning department (see Figures 1.1 and 1.4).

4. *What is the first task of the planning department manager in preparing the future firm?*
   The first task of the planning department manager in preparing the future firm is to work together with the firm's president in building the planning manual. This document specifies who?, what for?, when?, where? and how?, in other words, details concerning the meetings to plan the future firm. That is, who will take part in the meetings to evaluate present strategy, generate alternatives, approve the new organizational chart and so on and when and where those meetings will take place. An example of a planning manual is presented in Table 2.1. The front page shows who will participate in which decisions. Several aspects are worthy of note:

   - The decisions listed in columns correspond to the major steps in planning the future firm which will be addressed in Chapters 3 to 8.
   - The lines represent the top management levels of the firm.
   - The top of each line indicates who decides, the bottom, the extent of the participation. Therefore, the line in the first column indicates that this first decision will be ultimately taken by the president but he wishes to have meetings with his first management level. The president delegates decision 6C in Table 2.1 to the first management level and participation is extended down to the third management level. The ultimate decision on the overall budget, however, rests again with the president.

   The other pages of the planning manual must indicate for each meeting:

   - The agenda
   - The complete list of participants
   - Date and time (start and finish)

- The location: the firm's conference room, the president's office, or a hotel.

In short, the planning manual specifies the sequence of decisions to be taken; who will be present in the meetings (both who will be in charge and who will participate); the dates on which this will take place and the location. It is therefore a guide (a vade mecum) to take us through the whole process of managing the future firm.

5. *What is the role of the head of planning?*
As can be seen from the planning manual, it is the line managers who make the decisions.[8] Sometimes it is the president, at other times, the first level managers, and at yet others, the second level managers and so on, but never the head of planning. What is his role then? He has four roles: organizer, adviser, navigator and mechanic.

First, he prepares and organizes the meetings (agendas, locations), sends out the invitations and so on. Second, he sits in on all meetings and offers an opinion as and when necessary. Third, prior to the meetings, he provides all participants with the information required for decision making: the strategic plan drawn up last year; the industry segmentation matrixes to evaluate strategic alternatives; innovations suggested by the client analysis system; and so on. In short, all the information discussed in Chapters 3 to 8 (see Figure 2.4).

As a mechanic, the planning manager also has another function. Since the future firm is influenced not only by changes to what is done (effectiveness) but also the way in which these changes are made (efficiency), the planning manager acts as the leader of an internal task force which implements internal change (restructuring, mergers and so on) in the appropriate departments. Or he controls the work of external consultants on this matter, when applicable.

What he has to do and how he should act in his role as a mechanic is discussed in more detail in Chapter 9. This corresponds to step 7 in Figure 2.2 and involves improving efficiency in those departments:

- which are critical success factors in the firm's market segments (service, distribution, quality control, purchasing and so on)

Figure 2.4 The planning process

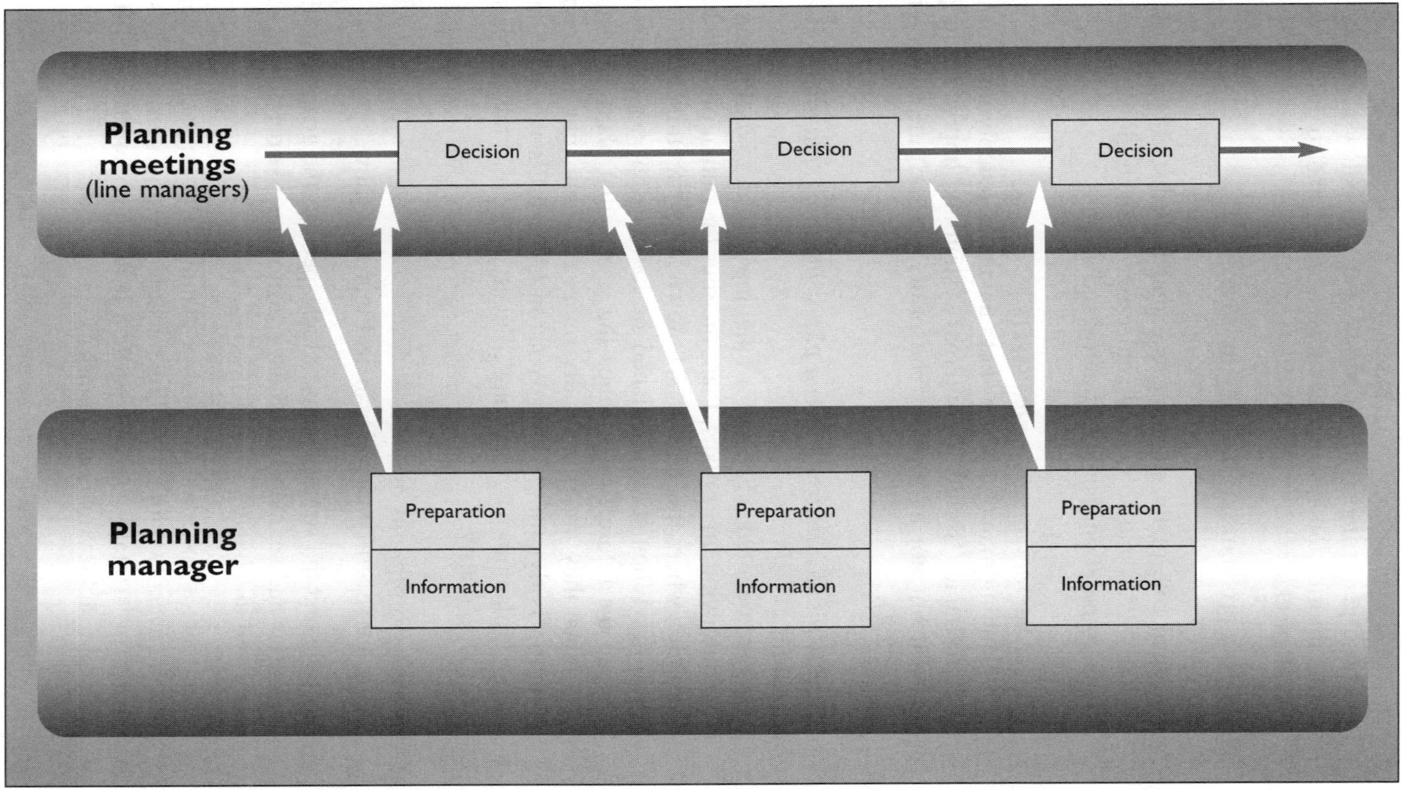

- whose performance the previous year was below acceptable levels (the information system, the merchandising and so on): the so-called bottlenecks
- where problems arise during the year.

The final role of the planning manager is to list all the plans of the various SBUs and so on and summarize them in global plans for the whole corporation: budget, strategy and so on.

6. *What is the role of the line managers?*
The planning manager acts as both navigator (supplying information) and mechanic ('fixing' the internal system and improving its performance), but not as a pilot. The pilots are the line managers (see Figure 2.4).

7. *What is the distinction between plans, planning, planning system and control?*
Plans are detailed schemes for attaining an objective. Planning is the actual drawing up of plans. Plans are thus the output of planning. (For example, when the author sat down to write this book he was planning. When it was finished he had written a plan on how to manage the future firm.) Hence the saying that plans are static, but that, since they are periodically reviewed (rethought and rewritten), planning is dynamic. Or in Winston Churchill's words: 'Plans are nothing; planning is everything'. Finally, control is the comparison of plans with reality.

8. *What types of plans are there?*
There are several types of plan, as Figure 2.5 shows.

   There is first the strategic plan, which specifies the geographical areas, industries and segments in which a firm wants to operate. This will be discussed in Chapter 3.

   Then there is so-called long-range planning (the subject of Chapter 8) which covers two topics: setting the objectives for a firm and its SBUs (if a firm is totally specialized then it is equivalent to an SBU) (for example achieving one-month average for receiving invoices,

Figure 2.5 Types of plan

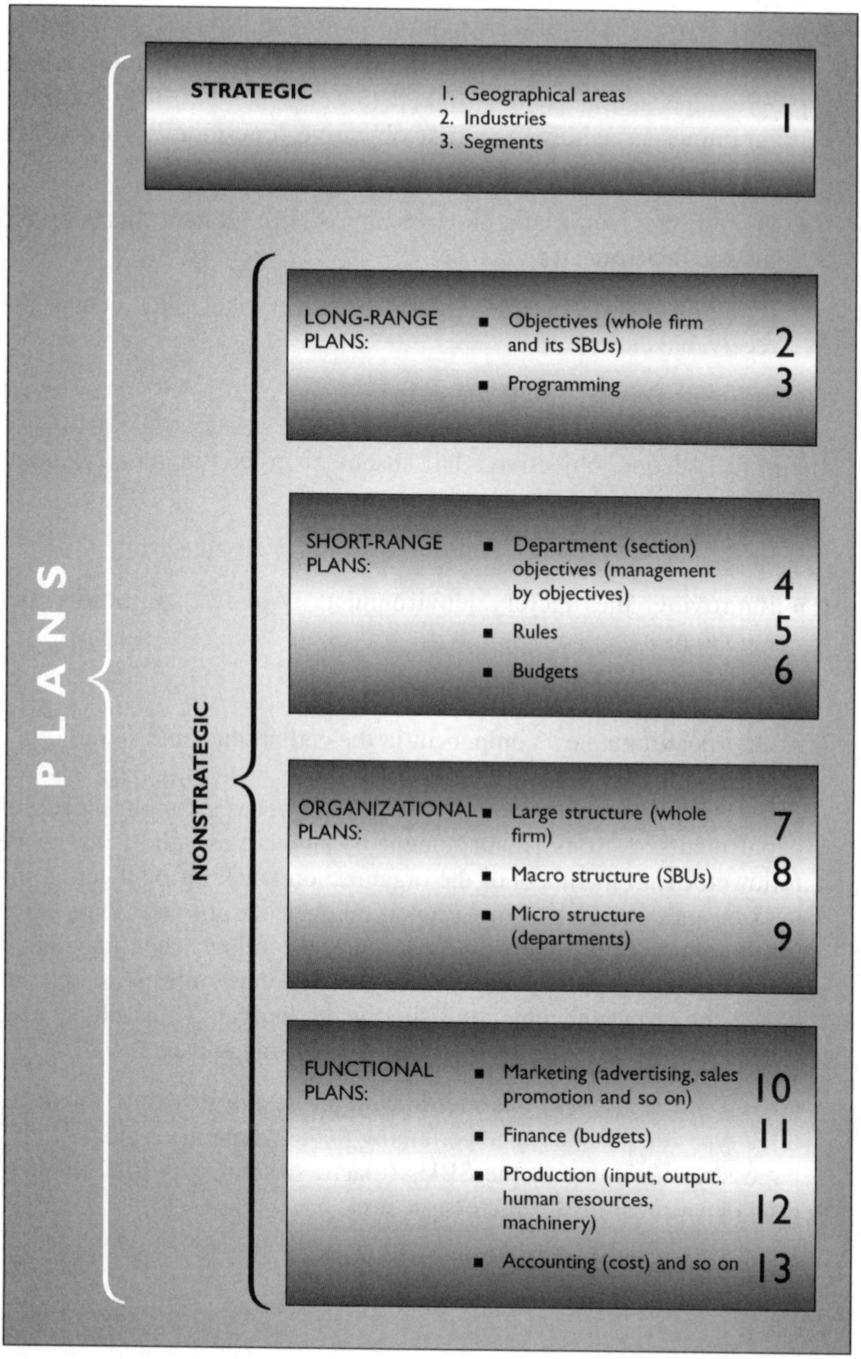

decreasing absenteeism to 3% in the factory, reducing the number of product defects to one-and-a-half per thousand, achieving a return on investment of 12% and so on) and programming – planning which programmes/actions will be taken to achieve them. For example, programmes to achieve the first objective (one-month average for receivables) could be:

- in the future requiring a previous approval of all new clients by the finance department(s)
- changing the salespeople's bonus so that it takes into account the receivable dates
- making receiving a function of the salespeople.

For the second objective, 3% absenteeism in the factory, other programmes could be designed:

- increasing the presence bonus to discourage absenteeism
- improving the factory environment – noise, pollution and ergonomics
- changing the quality control system
- incorporating a new component in the end product and so on.

Short-range planning includes setting objectives for the heads of departments/sections (management by objectives), the rules to be followed by all members of the organization when hiring a car, going on a business trip, choosing a hotel, number of split vacations which can be taken during the year, procedures to follow when handling a given machine (the document which contains these rules is sometimes called the 'vade mecum') and finally the budget. Thus, objectives, rules and budgets are the three types of short-range plans.

Organizational planning has to do with the design structure. There are three types of structure, one pertaining to the whole firm (the so-called large structure), one to the SBUs (macro structure) and the other to each department itself (micro structure).

Finally, there are the *functional plans* in marketing (advertising, merchandising and so on), in personnel, in accounting (the general plan is fixed by law to be the same for all firms but in cost accounting, each firm has freedom to plan as it likes), in production (forecasted outputs, inputs, machinery, personnel and so on). Some authors make an analogy between the firm's plans and the human body. The strategic plan behaves like the head providing vision (the eyes) and collecting information (the brain). The organizational plan is the skeleton. Long- and short-range plans are the nervous system carrying out the incentives. The functional plans are the muscle.

The functional plans cover the seven functional departments: production, finance, marketing, information system, accounting, administrative area (buildings maintenance, security, catering, office supplies purchases, communications and so on) and human resources.

Thus the *future* firm is built in two different ways: changes in the tasks to be carried out (segments, industries and geographical areas to be in), by the strategic planning. This is what to do. And changes in how to do those tasks. That is specified by long-range, short-range and organizational planning. The functional plans deal with the present, not the future firm.

9. *What emerges from planning*?
   Two things emerge from planning, a *revised strategy* and a *revised organization*. Following revision, one or both can be maintained or changed.

   The strategy, for example, will remain the same (*maintenance*) if no present market segment is abandoned after analysis in the examination matrix (see Figure 2.1) and no new market segment is adopted (because neither client analysis nor segmentation suggest any alternative or the suggested alternatives lack synergy).

   The new strategy will be of *concentration* if some segments are discontinued in the examination matrix but no new ones are adopted.

   The new strategy will focus on *expansion* if it is decided to maintain all present activities (market segments) and expand into new ones.

Finally, the new strategy can be a combination of concentration and expansion (old segments are abandoned and new ones entered into). In extreme cases, when the new strategy differs greatly from the previous one, this is known as a *turnaround* strategy (see Figure 2.6).[12]

10. *How long and often will the planning cycle (meetings to make the plans) last? Two months, four months, six months, or the whole year?* The answer is based on three factors. First, the planning cycle must cover a long series of decisions starting with defining and re-

Figure 2.6 Types of strategic decisions: comparing the new (future) with the old (present) strategy

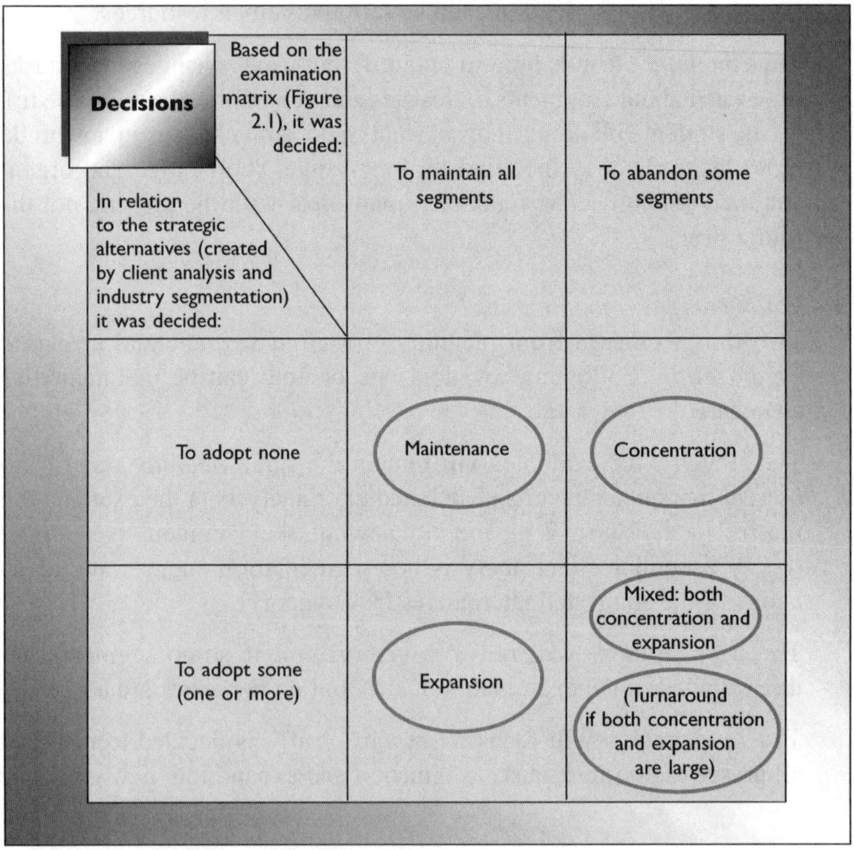

evaluating present strategy and ending with the budget (see Table 2.1). These decisions will be the contents of the plans referred in Figure 2.5, from strategic to organizational and functional.

Second, if the planning meetings are concentrated in a very short period of time (for example two months), during that period managers (for lack of time) will focus only on the future firm, neglecting the present one as a result. These two firms must always be managed simultaneously. Furthermore, there will be less time between meetings to read the information supplied by the planning manager and prepare for the meetings.

Third, smaller firms are less complex and therefore the preparation for the meetings and decision making requires less time.

In conclusion, the planning process seldom lasts less than three months (except, of course, in very small firms which can go through the whole cycle in one or two months) or more than six or seven months depending on the size of the corporation.

11. *How often should the cycle be repeated?*
One should note first of all that it is fundamental that the cycle of meetings be repeated periodically. That is what makes planning dynamic as opposed to plans which are static. Planning renews plans and prevents them from becoming obsolete. As Napoleon once said: 'bad is the plan which is not subject to revision'.

Therefore, some firms repeat the planning cycle every year and others every two years (only the budget is drawn up on a yearly basis). The choice depends on the degree of uncertainty present in the environment. If it is relatively stable, without major technological changes, changes in customer tastes and so on, then repeating the cycle every two years will suffice. If, however, there is great uncertainty and change, then a year-long planning cycle is required. Except for the budget, which should always be yearly, all other documents, strategic plans, long-range plans and so on can be drawn up every two years.

Thus, joining environmental uncertainty with company size, one must conclude that if both uncertainty and size are low, a three-month planning cycle (the period from the first until the last planning meeting) repeated every other year will suffice.

If, however, the company is large, then a longer planning cycle, say of six or seven months, is required.

Finally, if the firm is in a highly uncertain environment, then the planning cycle should be repeated every year and not every other year (see Figure 2.7).

12. *What characteristics should the planning cycle have?*
Regardless of the size of the firm and the characteristics of the environment, the planning cycle (meetings) should always have seven characteristics:

    1 All decisions are taken by line managers.

    2 The appropriate information must be supplied beforehand by the planning manager.

    3 It is important that there is at least a certain degree of participation from lower hierarchical levels.

    4 Total support by the president, which means participation in appropriate meetings and penalizing those managers who fail to participate when they are expected to.

    5 Planning should be repetitive (the planning cycle should be repeated every year or two years).

    6 Planning should be extended over some months (not concentrated in just a few).

    7 The sequence of decisions should be as shown in Table 2.1, from the definition and evaluation of present strategy through to preparation of the budget.

13. *Prior to making the planning department operational, what was done?*
Before the implementation of a planning department, only functional plans and budgeting, sometimes the vade mecum, and short-range objectives, were decided on a permanent and consistent basis.

Figure 2.7 How frequent and how long should the planning cycle be?

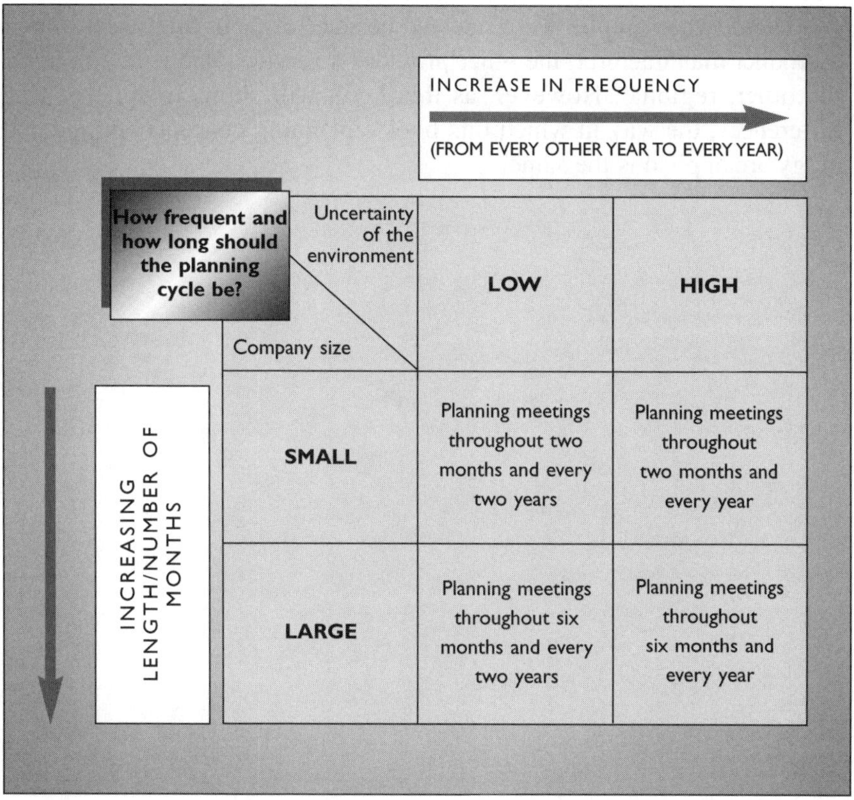

The rest (strategy, long-range planning and so on) was probably not carried out systematically. Therefore, the firm was not only unable to guarantee that each decision per se was optimized, but also that these decisions were mutually consistent and compatible.

In Chapters 3 to 9, each planning step of Table 2.1 will be analysed in detail. The output of each step is drawn in the plans listed in Figure 2.5.

To illustrate the practicality of this method, we shall follow two examples from start to finish in this book. They are two firms with very distinct products and strategies, Saab, the Swedish car manufacturer, and Caja de Madrid, a major Spanish financial institution.

These two examples were selected because of their differences. One is a product manufacturer, the other provides a service. One is international, the other, regional. However, as this book will show, in spite of their differences, the way in which this book's planning concepts and methodology are applied is the same.

CHAPTER 3

Step 1: Defining the Present Strategy

Introduction

There are two types of strategies: the present one and the future one. Frequently, there is a third type: what the firms' managers think their strategy is, which often has nothing to do with what the present strategy really is.

The *present strategy* is where the firm invoices, where its clients are, in actual, real terms. The *geographical areas* – New Hampshire, South Dakota, the whole of the US, or just New England; the *industries* – transport vehicles, software, real estate, or pharmaceutical products; and the *segments* in which the firm operates – subcompacts, compacts, overcompacts, luxury cars, buses, motorbikes, vans, station wagons and so on.

Then there is the *future strategy*, which is the market positioning that the firm wishes to achieve in the future. That is the reason why one makes a plan: the strategic plan detailing where it wants to go (geographical areas, industries and segments).[10]

As discussed in the previous chapter, present and future strategy can be totally equal (maintenance strategy) or very different (turnaround strategy). However, most real life situations imply smaller changes and fall in between the two. Future strategy will differ somewhat from present strategy. In any case, since only change is constant, present strategy must be periodically reviewed because what is adequate today may be inadequate tomorrow and obsolete the day after tomorrow.[11]

The starting point for planning

The starting point of the planning process must be the present strategy. That is, one must start the planning process by looking at where we are and then move on from there. One must not start anywhere else, for example by looking at the fastest growing areas in the economy, for one simple, fundamental reason. Present strategy and the firm's clients are what are paying the firm's salaries. How it is making a living. So before one starts looking for new markets, one should take a serious look at the present market position and see if it is worthwhile changing the old for the new, the certain for the uncertain.

Since present strategy is where a firm has its experience, it must therefore be the starting point of the planning process. Whether it will also be the final destination or not is a totally different question. But that is also the reason why one goes through the planning process. Naturally this does not apply in the case of a totally new firm. In such a case, the first step should be to segment the industry one wishes to be in, and then to select one or more segments based on strengths compared with the competition and the attractiveness of the various segments (growth perspectives, margin and sales volume).

The present strategy is found either in the latest strategic planning (carried out one or two years ago) or in the invoice files of the firm. The second option is always better, since the strategic plan indicates what one *wanted* to achieve, but the reality may be somewhat different. In fact, a firm can actually be in industry segments slightly different from those planned, or the segments may be precisely those planned but their turnover has not achieved that forecasted by the strategic plan.

Between aims and actions, plans and reality, there are frequently differences, and so one must start with the facts. Information regarding the facts, in other words present strategy, should be collected in an orderly way.[13]

The first step is to draw the industry segmentation matrix for each geographical area in which the firm operates, as indicated in Figure 3.1,[14] which presents an example from a leasing company. Listed are the various industry segments and how much the company invoices in each. Thus, naturally, the numbers in Figure 3.1 add up to 100%. Information will then be collected from the accounting system regarding the firm's turnover in each segment.

Figure 3.1 Present strategy of United Leasing & Co.

I

Geographical area: Canada
Industry: Leasing
Industry segmentation matrix

Clients \ Type of product	Fittings leasing		Real estate leasing	
	Productive equipment	Transport vehicles	Shops, offices and warehouses	Housing
Firms	1 20%	2 25%	3 10%	
Private	4	5		6
Managers, entrepreneurs and skilled professionals	7 15%	8 20%	9 10%	10
Public institutions	11	12	13	

II

Geographical area: Canada
Industry: Leasing
Industry segmentation matrix

Clients \ Type of product	Fittings leasing		Real estate leasing	
	Productive equipment	Transport vehicles	Shops, offices and warehouses	Housing
Firms	1	2 15%	3 20%	
Private	4	5		6
Managers, entrepreneurs and skilled professionals	7 10%	8 20%	9 20%	10 15%
Public institutions	11	12	13	

Present segments and % of company's turnover
Segments in which the firm is not present
Empty cells (non-existent segments)

That is the firm's present strategy: where it is invoicing and who its clients are. As Clausewitz, the great interpreter of Napoleon once said, 'strategy is where your army is and how strong it is'. In business terms this is where one's resources are, and where one invoices.

One should note that, as Figure 3.1 shows, the industry segmentation should be repeated for every geographical area. First, because an organization can be in different industries in different geographical areas (for example real estate in the US and public works in Canada, or pulp and paper in Brazil and wood in Europe and so on).

Second, even when the industries are the same, they can have some segments which are specific to certain geographical areas. For instance, in countries such as Portugal, Greece and Turkey, banking segmentation matrixes should include two special segments. The first is emigrants, who send their economies to their home country, sometimes accounting for 20–25% or more of total deposits. Another special segment is tourism, now in the corporate banking segmentation matrix. Tourism firms in this segment have special needs since their activity is largely cyclical.

Finally, even when the industry is the same in several geographic areas and there is no difference between the segmentation matrixes (no special segments), a firm can be in the same or different segments in distinct geographical areas. That is the case in Figure 3.1, which represents the strategy of a leasing company in two distinct markets, the US and Canada.[15]

In fact, United Leasing & Co. share segments 2, 3, 7, 8 and 9 between the US and Canada. However, the firm is also present in segment 1 (productive equipment for firms) in the US, while in Canada it is not. And in Canada it operates in segment 10 (homes for managers, entrepreneurs and skilled professionals) while in the US it does not.

Whatever the case (one or more geographical areas; same or different industries; same or different segmentation matrix; same or different segments), a firm's strategy is defined by the segments within industries and within geographical areas in which the organization operates.

The example of a leasing company was used to stress the universality of the concepts and methodology presented in this book. Henceforth, however, we will concentrate on our two main examples: Saab and Caja de Madrid. Although data on these two firms was consulted in order to make the examples as accurate and realistic as possible, several assumptions

BOX 3.1

This is the standard segmentation matrix for transportation vehicles. However, like any matrix, it can be enlarged to accommodate niches, using variables such as sex (for example the Toyota Corolla XLI is geared to the young housewife from classes A and B), age (for example the Nissan Micra for women in their 30s from class A), special needs (safety – Volvo), power (especially important in motorbikes whose power ranges from 50cc up to 1000cc, and more and so on). The luxury car segment can also be divided by price: up to US$40,000, between $40,000 and $80,000 and over $80,000; the sports car segment includes one niche up to $80,000, the next over $80,000 and so on.

regarding their competitive position, synergy and so on were also made. These are mere hypotheses with the single purpose of illustrating the concepts and methodology adopted. The aim was to optimize the power of the examples, not their accuracy.

BOX 3.2

Marketers usually distinguish among six different social classes: A, B, C1, C2, D and E; depending on income bracket and level of education. Families in social class E earn no more than 10% of two minimum wages (assuming two adults work) and generally possess the minimum education obligatory under the law. Social class A corresponds to the top 10% of families, in terms of income earned. Other classes fall in between.

Also, families go through different life phases: young singles; just married (no children); first nest (older child is below three years); full nest (older child is three or more years old); empty nest (first child at university); old single (no children or divorced); retired (one or both of the couple is retired); and survivor (only one of the couple is alive).

So 5% of Caja's sales are to just married couples, social class C1; 15% to first nest couples, social classes C1, C2 and D; 30% to full nest couples, C1, C2 and D classes and so on (Figure 3.3a).

Figures 3.2a, 3.2b and 3.3 illustrate the present strategy of Saab and Caja de Madrid.[16] The numbers within each cell (segment) indicate the real turnover they achieved as a percentage of the total company turnover.

Saab's strategy includes subcompacts (the 9-1 model) for social classes B and C1, overcompacts (the 9-3 sedan), station wagons (the 9-5 wagon)

Figure 3.2a Saab's real strategy (US)

I — US market Industry: Transport vehicles

Type of Car / Client	Social classes						Organizations
	A	B	C1	C2	D	E	Public/private
Motorbikes							
Subcompacts		Saab 9-1 3%					
Compacts							
Overcompacts	Saab 9-3 sedan 15%						
Station wagons	Saab 9-5 wagon 10%						
Vans (and light trucks)							
Luxury	Saab 9-5 sedan 5%						
Sports							
Mini-buses							
Buses							
Cargo							
Special purpose vehicles (4-wheel drive, armoured)							

Notes

1. [Number] Segments Saab is in. Numbers within each cell indicate *real* turnover as a percentage of total (100%) turnover
2. [ ] Segments Saab is not in
3. [shaded] Empty segments (nonexistent)

Figure 3.2b Saab's real strategy (EU)

II

EU market Industry: Transport vehicles

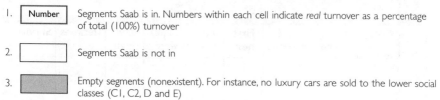

Type of Car \ Client	Social classes A	B	C1	C2	D	E	Organizations Public/private
Motorbikes							
Subcompacts		Saab 9-1 10%					
Compacts							
Overcompacts	Saab 9-3 sedan 24%						
Station wagons	Saab 9-5 wagon 18%						
Vans (and light trucks)							
Luxury	Saab 9-5 sedan 15%						
Sports							
Mini-buses							
Buses							
Cargo							
Special purpose vehicles (4-wheel drive, armoured)							

Notes

1. [Number] Segments Saab is in. Numbers within each cell indicate *real* turnover as a percentage of total (100%) turnover
2. [white box] Segments Saab is not in
3. [grey box] Empty segments (nonexistent). For instance, no luxury cars are sold to the lower social classes (C1, C2, D and E)

and the luxury (9-5 sedan), all for social classes A and B (see Box 3.1). The strategic segments are the same in the USA and Europe. However, Saab's turnover in Europe is far higher than in the USA, 67% versus 33%, indicating differences in their geographic strategy, which is also close to reality.

Figure 3.3 Caja de Madrid's real strategy

(a) Geographical area: Spain   Activity: Retail banking

Social class \ Life cycle	Young single	Just married	First nest	Full nest	Empty nest	Old single	Retirees	Survivors
A								
B								
C1		5	4	11	8	6	3	1
C2			6	10	8	7	3	1
D			5	9	7	4	1	1
E								

Notes

1. [Number] Segments Caja de Madrid is in. Numbers within each cell indicate *real* turnover as a percentage of total (100%) turnover
2. [ ] Segments Caja de Madrid is not in
3. Young singles = unmarried customers
   Just married = married couples with no children
   First nest = older child is three or less years old
   Full nest = older child is three or more years old
   Empty nest = at least one child at college (leaving home or not)
   Old single = no children or divorcees
   Retirees = one or both of the couple is retired
   Survivors = only one of the couple is alive

(b) Main four market areas occupied by Caja

Social class \ Life cycle	Young single	Just married	First nest	Full nest	Empty nest	Old single	Retirees	Survivors
A								
B								
C1								
C2								
D								
E								

In each of these segments, Saab achieves a certain turnover: 3% in subcompacts for classes B and C1; 15% overcompacts in social classes A and B; and so on (see Box 3.2).

To simplify, we can classify the segments in which Caja operates in four major groups as shown in Figure 3.3b:

- Young singles/just married and social class C1;
- First nest/full nest and social classes C1, C2 and D;
- Empty nest/old singles and social classes C1, C2 and D;
- Retirees/survivors and social classes C1, C2 and D.

These four major groupings will be used in the rest of the book.

Having defined the present (real) strategy of our company, we are ready for the next step: to evaluate it. The question is: Should we continue in all our segments or just a few? And, if so, in which? And why? That is answered in the following chapter.

CHAPTER 4

Step 2: Evaluating the Present Strategy

Introduction

Having defined the present strategy, the question is: should the organization maintain all or just a few of its present segments and discontinue operations in others and if so, which? In order to decide, the present segments that the firm occupies should be evaluated. Although this was done one or two years ago, when the firm last made its present strategic plan, it is now time to repeat the process.

Indeed, everything changes (except human nature). New competitors may have entered market segments; other competitors may have left; technology may have changed and also consumer tastes. New segments may have emerged, eroding the present customer base, and the organization's strengths may have changed, and so on.

Since nothing is permanent except change, where our firm stands at a given moment must be periodically evaluated. There are two criteria for such an evaluation: *attractiveness* and *competitive position*.

Attractiveness

Attractiveness[17] means:

1. *Volume* of foreseeable sales in the segment;

2. The *margin* it is hoped will be achieved per unit of the product sold;
3. The *growth rate* over the next three to five years.

Naturally enough, the greater these values, the more attractive the segment will be. In practice, some segments will be more attractive, others less so. Therefore it is useful to group the three values, the attractiveness variables, under just one value. This can be done by using the variable profit (in absolute values) or profitability (in return on investment (ROI) terms – investment profitability). The investment can be assets (return on assets) or equity (return on equity). In the first case, either the cumulative value for a period of three to five years or for this period can be used. In the second case, the average year value should be used (see Box 4.1). The three options are shown in Figure 4.1. Even if not exactly equivalent, they produce similar results in practical terms.

In order to summarize the three variables in a single variable one applies the following formula[18] – unit margin multiplied by sales volume equals total margin. By applying the forecast year market growth rate to the total margin, one obtains how the total margin will evolve in the next period (say the next three or five years). Adding up all the years provides the cumulative profit for the period (cell 2 in Figure 4.1). Then, if one divides that cumulative profit by the number of years in the period, one has the average year profit (cell 1 in Figure 4.1). That year profit divided by

BOX 4.1

A good book on marketing or a basic book on strategy contains several methods for estimating sales, margin and the growth rate of any given segment. Indeed, marketing books present various evaluation methods such as:[19] the method of the channels of distribution; evaluations based on similar products; the international product life cycle (where countries come in different phases due to being in diverse development stages and thus some countries can be used as predictors to others); time series and regression analysis (to forecast growth rates) and so on, as well as official statistics or information provided by specialized private firms such as Nielsen, Girassic, DBK. Because these methods are reasonably presented in any good marketing book, there is no need to develop them here.

the amount to be invested (total assets or equity) gives the return on assets or equity. That is the return on investment of cell 3 of Figure 4.1.

The attractiveness variables need summarizing in a single index (1, 2 or 3 in Figure 4.1) because they are not perfectly correlated: one segment can rate higher in one variable and lower in another, or vice versa. However, generally there is a relationship between the three variables and this is indicated in Figure 4.2.

As Figure 4.2 shows, there is generally a positive relation between profit margin and the rate of market growth (the higher one of them, the higher the other tends to be), and a negative relation in all cases (that is, as one variable increases, the other decreases and vice versa).

The reasons are:

1. Higher rates of growth are usually found in the early phases of the product life cycle, when sales volume is lower. Thus, a negative relation occurs in cells 2 and 4.
2. Mature markets (lower rates of growth) tend to be more competitive. Consequently, in general there is a positive relation between growth

Figure 4.1 Four ways of combining the three variables of attractiveness

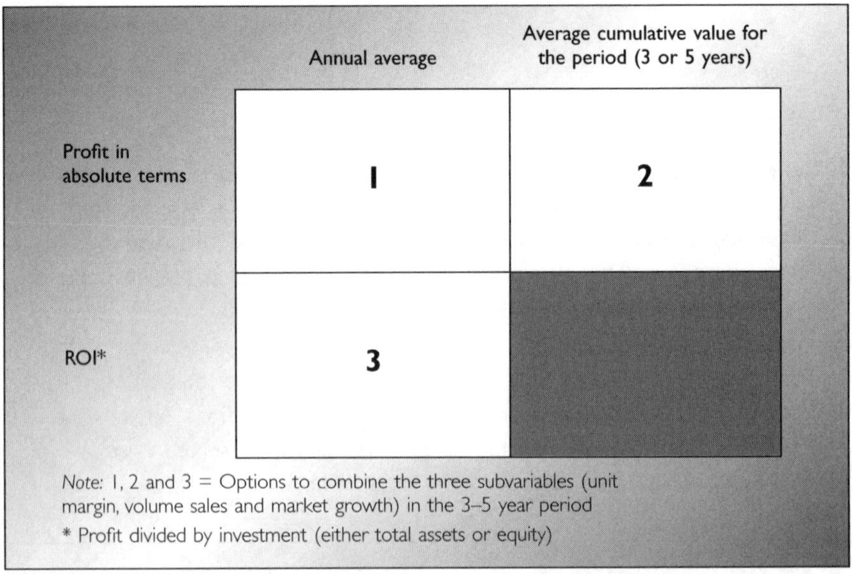
Annual average
Average cumulative value for the period (3 or 5 years)
Profit in absolute terms
ROI*
1
2
3

Note: 1, 2 and 3 = Options to combine the three subvariables (unit margin, volume sales and market growth) in the 3–5 year period
* Profit divided by investment (either total assets or equity)

Figure 4.2 Correlations among attractiveness variables

Correlation between variables within *any* segment X	Sales volume	Rate of growth	Profit margin
Sales volume	1.	4. Negative	7. Negative
Rate of growth	2. Negative	5.	8. Positive
Profit margin	3. Negative	6. Positive	9.

Notes:
1. Negative means: they move in opposite ways (when one increases, the other decreases, and vice versa)
2. Positive means: they move in the same way (when one increases, so does the other; when one decreases, the other does too)

rate and profit margin (less competition) in cells 6 and 8. That is, low growth rate (mature markets) → high level of competition → low profit margin.

3. There is a negative relation between sales volume (mature markets) and profit margins (cells 3 and 7).

Relations 1, 2 and 3 are general. However, in each specific situation the concrete (negative or positive) value of the correlation will vary. But since the variables are not perfectly related, they must be summarized in one of the three ways indicated in each of the cells of Figure 4.1. Multiplying unit margin by unit sales by market growth, one obtains a measure of attractiveness.

Competitive position

The second criteria for evaluating present strategy is the competitive position[20] of the firm in each segment. Indeed, the attractiveness (or profitability) of the segment is important but it is an average estimate for the segment. For example, it might be estimated that a segment would grow on average between 4% and 6% in the next three to five years. Some firms, however, will grow more and others less. Some firms will be above the average, others below. That is why information on the average segment attractiveness must be complemented by information on the competitive position of the company in that market segment. If it has competitive superiority, it will be above the average, if it has competitive inferiority, it will be below the average.

The competitive position of a company stems from the qualities/strengths and defects/weaknesses that it possesses in its critical success factors.[21]

Let us start with these. In any segment, an organization must perform dozens of tasks satisfactorily to serve the client. It has to offer high quality products, a good image and suitable distribution channels; it must have reasonably sophisticated equipment in technological terms; it must have motivated, skilled and satisfied factory workers; the location of its factories must be appropriate; the product development and quality control departments must perform well; the sales force must have good technical and marketing knowledge; and so on.

All of this is important. Nevertheless, empirical evidence shows that, in order to achieve superior performance, there are some tasks which are more important than others for each market segment. The most important tasks are called critical success factors. (There are four basic methods for finding critical success factors: path analysis; risk analysis; client analysis; and decision analysis. Since they are thoroughly explained elsewhere,[27] they will not be developed here. For those interested in the subject see, for example, *The Modern Alchemists.*[22]) To paraphrase George Orwell, *all the variable tasks are equally important for good performance, but some are more important than others.*

For example, as Figure 4.3 indicates, the critical success factors in subcompact cars are price, consumption, manoeuvrability and design. Price is critical because, as subcompacts are small cars, the customer uses them mostly as an utilitarian vehicle and is therefore less eager to pay the price for higher quality features. Consumption and manoeuvrability are also important since it is an urban car. Finally, design is frequently a distinctive characteristic.[23] These variables, which are extremely important in terms of performance in a given sector of the market, are called critical success factors. In each market segment, there are generally three, four or five critical success factors.

Figure 4.3 Competitive position of Saab's subcompact segment (EU)

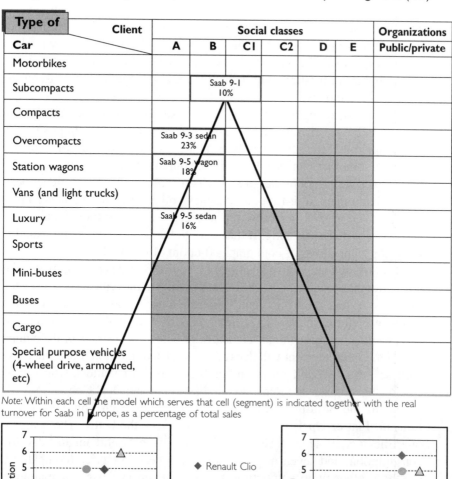

Type of Car / Client	Social classes A	B	C1	C2	D	E	Organizations Public/private
Motorbikes							
Subcompacts		Saab 9-1 10%					
Compacts							
Overcompacts	Saab 9-3 sedan 23%						
Station wagons	Saab 9-5 wagon 18%						
Vans (and light trucks)							
Luxury	Saab 9-5 sedan 16%						
Sports							
Mini-buses							
Buses							
Cargo							
Special purpose vehicles (4-wheel drive, armoured, etc)							

Note: Within each cell the model which serves that cell (segment) is indicated together with the real turnover for Saab in Europe, as a percentage of total sales

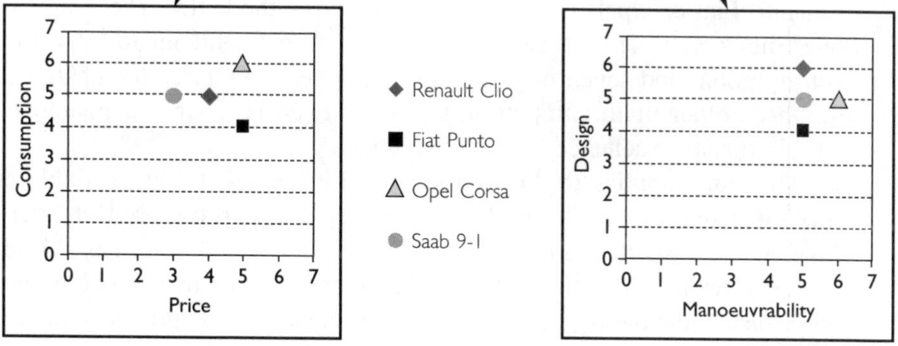

$$\text{Competitive position} = \frac{4.5 - \left(\frac{5.0 + 4.5 + 5.5}{3}\right)}{\left(\frac{5.0 + 4.5 + 5.5}{3}\right)} = -10\%$$

Where: 4.5 = Saab's 9-1 average in the four success factors
5.0 = Renault Clio's average in the four success factors
4.5 = Fiat Punto's average in the four success factors
5.5 = Opel Corsa's average in the four success factors

Note: 1 = poor, 7 = excellent

One should note that critical success factors are something belonging to an activity, whether it be business, sport, culture and so on. For example, one of the critical success factors in basketball is height; for a jockey it is weight (the lighter the better); for a Japanese sumo wrestler it is also weight (the heavier the better); in chess it is memory (of previous moves by grand masters) and deductive logic (to predict the consequence of alternative moves).[23]

In contrast, strengths (qualities) and weaknesses (faults) do not belong to an activity but to an entity (person, organization or country). In practice, no entity has only strengths or only weaknesses but a mixture of both. For example, some companies will offer more durable products than competitors but perhaps with a poorer design; some companies will achieve higher penetration than others in distribution channels; others may have a better image but be less competitive in terms of price; and so on. Therefore, in Figure 4.3, no firm is best at everything. If that were to happen, the company would be in the top right corner of both graphs (bottom of Figure 4.3).

The overall competitive position of a company is determined by whether it has strengths (qualities) or weaknesses (faults) in the critical success factors (the three or four most important variables in each market segment);[24] what its rating is (for example on a scale of one to seven) in the key variables for success; whether these ratings are above or below the average of the companies in the same segment will determine its relative position. For comparison purposes, usually one focuses on the three major competitors, which in the case of subcompacts are Renault Clio, Fiat Punto and Opel Corsa.

So in the bottom of Figure 4.3, the closer each company (Saab, Renault, Fiat or Opel) is to seven (in any axis), the better. The nearer to one, the worse. Thus a seven in consumption would mean very low consumption; and seven in price indicates a very low price (compared to the three other main competitors). And a seven in design or manoeuvrability means excellence in these variables.

The same applies to the examples in Figure 4.4. In any variable, a seven is a sign of excellence (high quality special purpose products, very easy access, excellent image of dynamism and very low prices – both interest rates and fees charged). On the other hand, a value of one in any scale means just the opposite: very weak special purpose products, highly difficult access, and so on.

It is possible to visualize the competitive position of a company using Cartesian graphs (see bottom of Figures 4.3 and 4.4), the axes of which

Figure 4.4 Competitive position of Caja de Madrid in segments C1, C2 and D, first and full nest

Caja de Madrid – real strategy

Social class \ Life cycle	Young single	Just married	First nest	Full nest	Empty nest	Old single	Retirees	Survivors
A								
B								
C1								
C2			1					
D								
E								

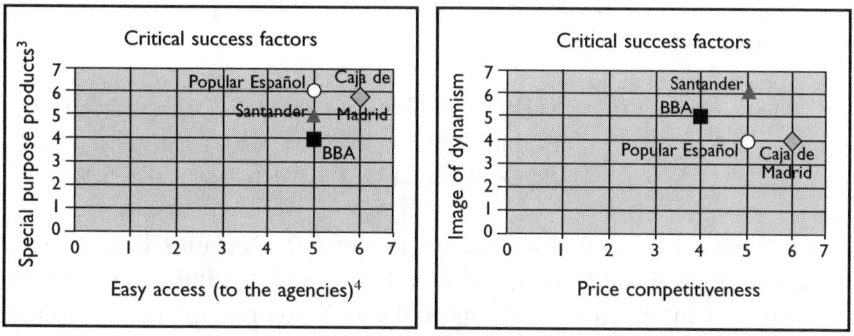

$$\text{Competitive position} = \frac{5.50 - \left(\frac{4.50 + 5.25 + 5.00}{3}\right)}{\left(\frac{4.50 + 5.25 + 5.00}{3}\right)} = \frac{5.50 - 4.92}{4.92} = +12\%$$

Where:
- 5.5 = Caja's average in the four success factors
- 4.5 = BBA's average in the four success factors
- 5.25 = Santander's average in the four success factors
- 5.0 = Popular Español's average in the four success factors

Notes:

1. In the scale, 7 means lowest interest rates and lower service fees; 1 means highest
2. BBA = Banco Bilbao y Argentaria
3. Loans for cars, furniture, and so on
4. Location and parking facilities

show ratings for different critical success factors. The specific position occupied by the firm (from one to seven) depends on how its strengths and weaknesses compare with those of the competition.

The three best competitors (those having a larger share of the market) in a certain segment are usually used as a yardstick for comparison, since using all the competition would be cumbersome and competitors with large shares are the most important. Some competitors are better in some areas than others.

The use of Cartesian graphs also enables this competitive position to be summarized in one average value. Thus, we can tell whether the company is below or above the average of its three best competitors.

To do this, one should proceed as follows. First one calculates the average marks of the company in each of the critical success factors. Saab's average is (3 in price + 5 in consumption + 5 in design + 5 in manoeuvrability)/4 variables = 4.5 and Caja de Madrid's average is (6 in special purpose products + 6 in easy access + 4 in images of dynamism + 6 in price competitiveness)/4 variables = 5.5.

Then do the same for each of the three main competitors in the relevant market segment.

Saab's competition: ◆ Renault Clio = (4 + 5 + 5 + 6) ÷ 4 = 5.0
■ Fiat Punto = (5 + 4 + 5 + 4) ÷ 4 = 4.5
△ Opel Corsa = (5 + 6 + 6 + 5) ÷ 4 = 5.5

Thus, Saab's competition has an average of 5.0 (Renault Clio), 4.5 (Fiat Punto) and 5.5 (Opel Corsa); adding all three and dividing by 3 = 5.0. By the same token, the average strength of Caja's competition has an average of 4.92: (4.5 + 5.25 + 5)/3.

Finally, to summarize the competitive position of the firms in terms of the competition, one must calculate the relative percentage that they are below or above the competitors: in the case of Saab: (4.5 of Saab average – 5.0 of competitor's average)/5.0 of competitor average = –10% and in Caja: (5.50 of Caja's average – 4.92 of competition's average)/4.92 of competition average = +12%.

In the subcompact segment, Saab therefore has on average 10% lower quality in the key success factors than the competition. In contrast, Caja de Madrid is 12% (on average) above the competition.

In other cases, the conclusion may have been different. One could have 15% more, 20% more or 5% or 10% less, which would all be possible values in other situations.

Thus, the competitive position figures are important in that they express as a simple percentage how the two firms compare with their main competitors in terms of strong and weak points in the critical success factors (Box 4.2). This should be done for all segments, as competitors, the key success factors and how our firm and their competitors rate will vary from segment to segment. So, each of Saab's and Caja de Madrid's present segments (Figures 3.2 and 3.3) should be evaluated in terms of attractiveness and the firm's competitive position within it (see Box 4.3).

The analysis can be carried out for each cell in Figures 4.3 and 4.4, in which our firm is present or, if there are no great differences between these cells, these can then be summarized in groups, for which the analysis is then carried out.

To simplify the process, the cells in Figures 3.2. and 3.3, Saab's social classes and vehicle type and Caja de Madrid's social classes and life-cycle stages will be grouped together and analysed.

BOX 4.2

To evaluate strengths and weaknesses there are six basic methods. The first uses simple measurements: for example the quality of location is measurable by distance to market and the extent of parking facilities; the quality of coal reserves by the level of sulphur, impurities and thickness; price is a straightforward variable evaluated through cross shopping; the quality of assistance can be judged through the number of customer complaints; product size (important in mobile phones for example) is easily measurable; and so on.

Other attributes can be evaluated by tests performed on the product, such as passenger or luggage space in cars, the level of fuel consumption, safety, speed; and so on.

The evaluation of other attributes (the quality of the image of a firm; the knowhow of its sales force) is subjective. There are four methods: the Delphi technique; the method without maximum; the technique without self-evaluation; and external panels. For those interested in pursuing the subject, please see the Notes at the end of the book.

BOX 4.3

> To simplify, each segment's attractiveness and competitive position in Europe and the US is considered to be similar. So, in the case of Saab, one evaluates only four (and not eight) market areas. In the real world, because the three largest competitors may be different in both markets, the competitive position will probably differ as well as the key success factors and attractiveness. Therefore, the analysis should be repeated for the US and Europe.

Consequently, the markets for Saab are:

Subcompacts	B C1
Overcompacts	A B
Station wagons	A B
Luxury cars	A B

And for Caja de Madrid the markets are:

Just married	C1
First nest Full nest	C1 C2 D
Empty nest Old singles	C1 C2 D
Retired Survivors	C1 C2 D

Figure 4.5 Saab's evaluation matrix (present strategy)

Source: Adapted from Aaker, D., *Stratgic Market Management*, 1998

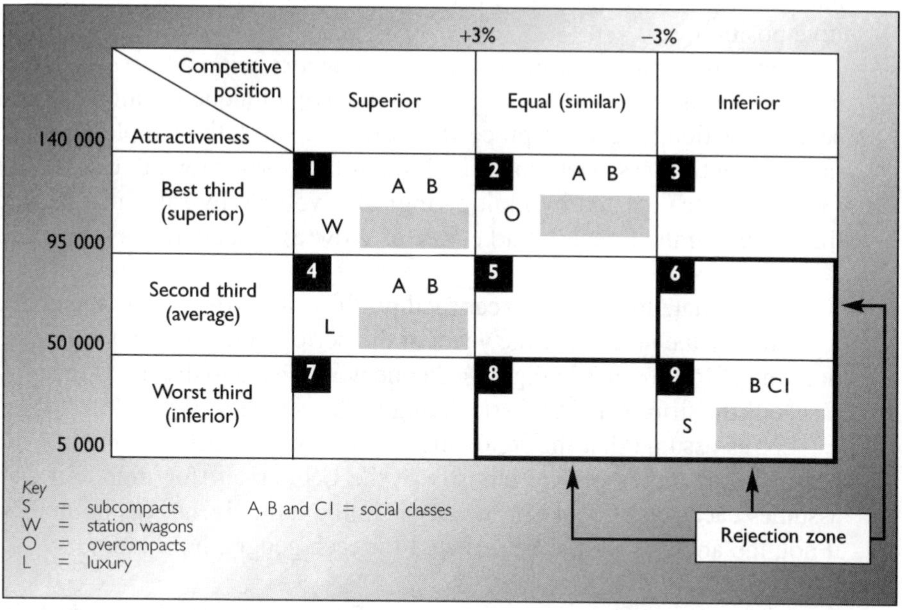

Figure 4.6 Caja de Madrid's evaluation matrix (present strategy)

Source: Adapted from Aaker, D., *Stratgic Market Management*, 1998

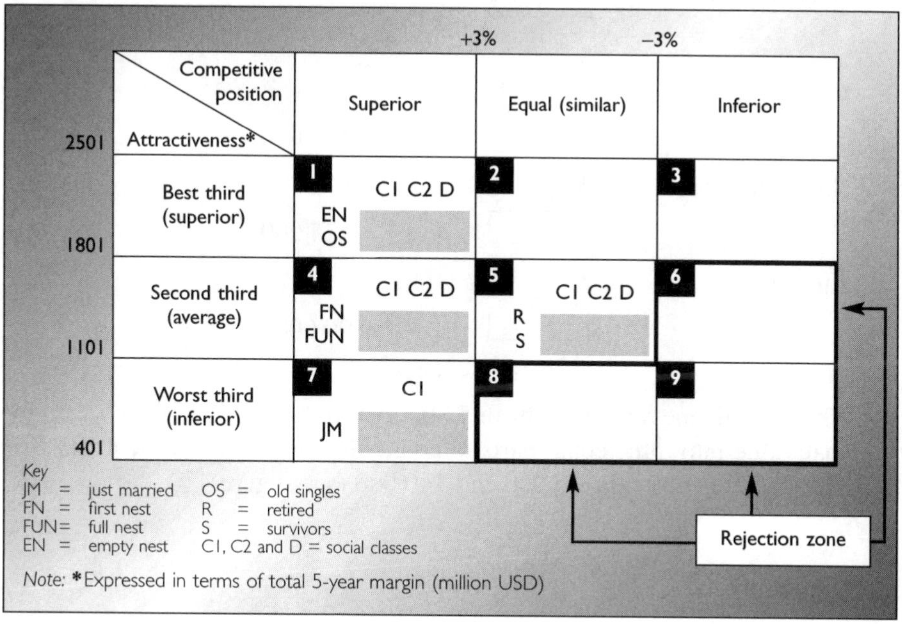

These market areas can be put in a 3 × 3 matrix as shown in Figures 4.5 and 4.6, where one dimension is attractiveness and the other the competitive position.

Segments (market areas) *can fall anywhere within this evaluation matrix*. But in practice, each segment will have a unique position. To find such a position, one must proceed as follows. First, the simplest way to make attractiveness operational is through total profit for the near future (3–5 years) (calculated by multiplying sales volume by sales margin and then applying the forecast market rate of growth). That corresponds to cell 2 in Figure 4.1.

To calculate the average year total profit (cell 1), one would then have to divide by the number of the years of the period (3 or 5). And to measure in terms of ROI (cell 3 in Figure 4.1) one would have to divide by the total assets of the firms (on SBUs) operating in the segment.

Let us assume that the following are the total expected profits for the period in the motor vehicle industry in the US market (for simplicity one assumes each segment in Europe has a similar attractiveness as in the US; if not, the analysis should be repeated for each geographical area):

Segments		*Total profits next 5 years in US$ millions (US market)*
Subcompacts	B C1 [1]	= 5 000
Overcompacts	A B [2]	= 140 000
Station wagons	A B [3]	= 125 000
Luxury cars	A B [4]	= 90 000

The attractiveness range is from 5 000 to 140 000 = 135 000. If we divide that value into three equal parts to create the three lines of the evaluation matrix, we get 50 000, 95 000 and 140 000 (see Figure 4.5).

For Caja de Madrid one has, for example:

Segments		*Total margin next 5 years in US$ millions (Spanish market)*
Just married	C1	= 401
First nest Full nest	C1 C2 D	= 1781
Empty nest Old singles	C1 C2 D	= 2501
Retired Survivors	C1 C2 D	= 1104

Therefore the dividing lines to form the three tiers are 1101, 1801 and 2501 (see Figure 4.6). If one worked with return on assets (cell 3 in Figure 4.1) instead of total profits, then the dividing line between the third and second line would be the cost of funding. The dividing line between the first and second line would be the average value between the cost of funding and the return of the best segment.

Second, one must calculate each segment/market area's competitive position as in Figures 4.3 and 4.4. Let us assume that the four Saab areas are (from lowest to highest competitive position):

−10% for subcompacts for classes B and C1
+2% for overcompacts for classes A and B
+4% for station wagons for classes A and B
+6% for luxury cars for classes A and B

And for Caja de Madrid (again, from lowest to highest competitive position):

−2% for retired and survivors – C1, C2 and D
+6% for just married – C1
+10% for empty nest/old singles – C1, C2 and D
+12% for first nest/full nest – C1, C2 and D

Third, each segment now has a precise position in the evaluation matrix of Figures 4.5 and 4.6. For practical purposes, equal/similar is usually considered to be between –3% and +3%. Another cutoff point could be used, as long as it is not very different from zero.

Fourth, one can now see if any segment falls within the rejection area (cells 6, 8 and 9 in the lower right corner of the matrix). If it does, it means that the segment is either inferior in one area (attractiveness or competitive position) and average in the other or inferior in both. Saab has one such segment: subcompacts for classes B and C1, in cell 9, whereas Caja de Madrid has none.

Fifth, one of two things can happen in terms of segments which fall within the rejection zone. Either the division which is handling that segment is losing money and that segment's operations should be immediately phased out. Or, taking into account the average cost of funding including equity, and therefore the opportunity cost, it is making money, in which case it should be put on hold to see if a better alternative (a new segment) comes up later during the planning process where new alternatives are generated (the subject of Chapter 5). If so, the old segment should be discontinued in favour of the new ones. If not, it should be maintained.

Three questions are pertinent here. First, why not simply check to see if the division handling a given segment is profitable or not and discontinue it if appropriate? There are two reasons and the first is that it may be losing money because the segment's present sales and margin are low but the prospects are good. That is why it is necessary to take into account the market rate of growth and calculate the attractiveness value for the market for a 3–5 year period and not merely the current profitability of the division. The other reason is that losses may be due to temporary factors which will be overcome, such as accidents, strikes, breakdowns in supplies and so on, and not to structural factors which tend to endure strategic strengths and weaknesses. That is why the competitive position must be evaluated.

Second, one should note that, given the way the matrix is constructed, all segments must fall within the first, second or third column (to have superior, similar or inferior competitive position); and because the attractiveness range is divided into three equal intervals, at least one segment will fall in the bottom third (that of inferior attractiveness). This is deliberate as it offsets any tendency to overevaluate the competitive position and therefore increase the probability of some segments falling in the rejection area (two of the three cells of the bottom third fall in the rejection zone) (Box 4.4).

BOX 4.4

If strengths and weaknesses were evaluated using the appropriate methods (see Box 4.2), the risk of overstating the case for our competitive position is minimal. Thus an alternative to creating three equal intervals within the range between minimum and maximum profits (as in Figures 4.5 and 4.6) would be to create three lines based on: more than twice the cost of capital (top line); below the cost of capital (bottom line); and in between, as shown below.

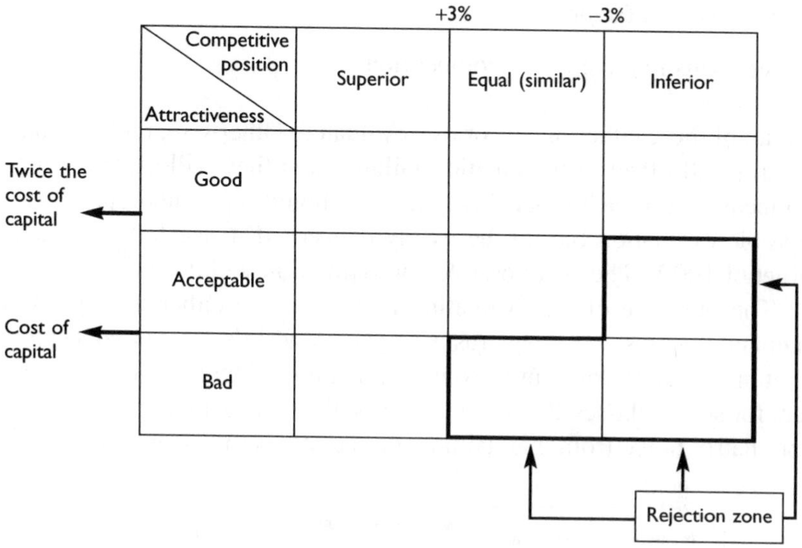

Experience shows that, in practical terms, this way of constructing the matrix or using total profits to separate the lines (as in the main text) provides similar, but not equivalent, results.

One should use one or the other, depending on how accurate one believes that the competitive position was evaluated. If one is uncertain, the method used in the main text is better. If one is reasonably certain, the method presented in this box is preferable.

Finally, one should try to evaluate carefully both attractiveness and competitiveness. However, approximations will suit our purpose since, in order to seriously misplace a segment in the evaluating matrix, there must have been a failure in the evaluation of:

- sales volume
- sales margin
- date of growth
- key success factors
- strengths relative to the competition

and all of these either under- or overevaluated. Otherwise, underevaluation failures will offset overevaluation failures, and they will therefore tend to compensate for each other. In short, one should try to undertake the best possible evaluation but not be overly concerned if one fails to reach the target of 100%. The best possible approximation will do.[25]

The outcome of the evaluating matrix can be either a suggestion to maintain the present strategy (as in Caja de Madrid's case) or concentration (if it suggests discontinuing some segments), as with Saab (subcompact cars for social classes B and C1). That is, the conclusions from the evaluation matrix range from maintaining all operations to discontinuing all.[26]

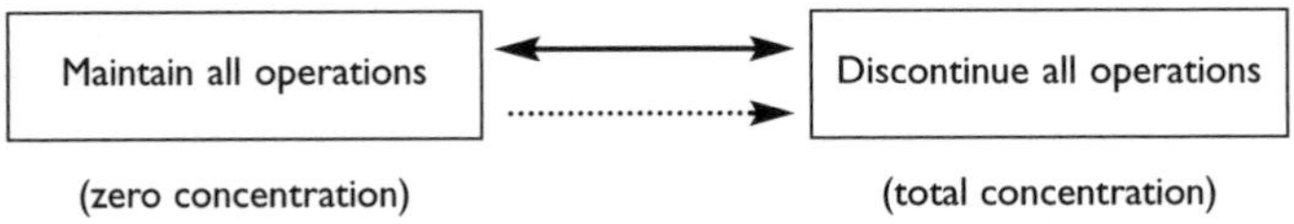

The degree of concentration along this continuum varies from a minimum of zero, in the case where all operations are maintained, to total (100%) concentration, if all operations are discontinued.

Thus, concentration can be low, when the number of segments in the rejection area of the matrix compared to the total number of segments is low, or high. In such a case, one speaks of a turnaround strategy. Two measures of the degree of concentration are the number of segments to be abandoned divided by the total number of segments and what those segments represent in the firm's total turnover.

Whatever the situation, however, so far we have merely evaluated present strategy. Any corporation can operate in many other segments, where at present it does not. Those segments constitute alternatives to present activities. Therefore they must first be created and then evaluated to see if they are worthwhile. That is the task of the next chapters: Chapter 5 – Generating Strategic Alternatives and Chapter 6 – Evaluating the Strategic Alternatives.

CHAPTER 5

Step 3: Generating Strategic Alternatives

Introduction

Outside present strategy there is a world of potential opportunities to exploit.[27] The aim of this chapter is to introduce two methods, client analysis and segmentation, which are most likely to produce interesting results.

Client analysis

Client analysis is market research on present clients. Some of the market research methods and firms which use them are shown in Table 5.1.

One may ask: why focus on present clients? First, because they are a source of opportunities. Second, because opportunities which come from them have a greater chance of success. Indeed, a corporation has greater credibility with its present clients. They are paying the firm's salaries. So why not use them as the inspiration for new ventures?[28]

Firms should consequently use some or all of the methods every three or six months in Table 5.1 to collect information, and then draw up a report (summarized on a yearly basis) comprising four sections. Each section contains answers to a specific question and constitutes a given set of opportunities (see Figure 5.1).[29]

The first section of the report answers the question: who is our client? When the firm's clients are people, this involves defining social class,

Table 5.1 Some market research methods for client analysis

Methods	Firms which use them
1 Reports filled in by employees acting as clients	TWA, Warner Electric, Digital, Estée Lauder, and so on
2 Questionnaires to clients	McDonald's, Kentucky F.C., IBM, Purdue firms, British Airways, Metro/Makro, Domino's Pizza, and so on
3 Problem research: interviews with small groups of clients which, focusing on the firm's products, list: 1. their problems 2. how important they are 3. the degree to which a solution exists: The degree of opportunity equals: 1 × 2 × 3	Avis, City Trust, Toyota, Fuji, Nissan, and so on
4 Benefit analysis: interviews with larger client groups (40–50 persons) which list: 1. benefits sought in the product 2. degree to which the organization satisfies it The opportunity = 1 × 2	Sakura, Honda, Philips, Siemens, Gerber, Boehringer Manheim, American Express, and so on
5 Nonstructured interviews: groups of 6–10 people with which past experience and new ways of using the products are discussed freely	Nestlé, Hewlett-Packard, Johnson & Johnson, Procter & Gamble, and so on
6 Free telephone number for clients	Coca-Cola, IBM, Casio, ATT, and so on
7 Suggestion boxes for clients and employees	Toyota, Mitsubishi, Suzuki, and so on
8 Simulation (a group of clients design their ideal product or store)	Marks & Spencer, Printemps, Sears, Wall-Mart, and so on

phase of life cycle (from young singles to retired persons) and their cultural and demographic characteristics: sex, urban-suburban-rural, race and political leaning. When clients are firms (generally, a firm who sells to people manufactures consumer goods; and a firm who sells to firms produces industrial goods), the most frequently used variables are size, type (public, private), nationality (especially relevant for international firms) and industry (plastics, software, ceramics, insurance; and so on).

By defining who buys from our firm, one is defining who does not buy from it, and all these constitute potential opportunities.[30] Two situations

Figure 5.1 Client analysis report

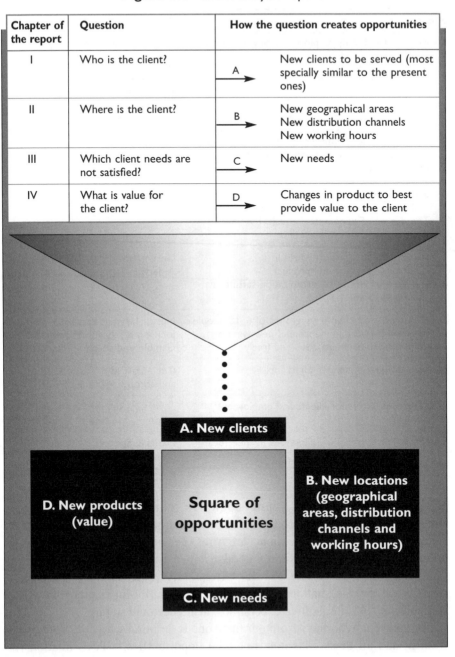

Chapter of the report	Question	How the question creates opportunities
I	Who is the client?	A → New clients to be served (most specially similar to the present ones)
II	Where is the client?	B → New geographical areas New distribution channels New working hours
III	Which client needs are not satisfied?	C → New needs
IV	What is value for the client?	D → Changes in product to best provide value to the client

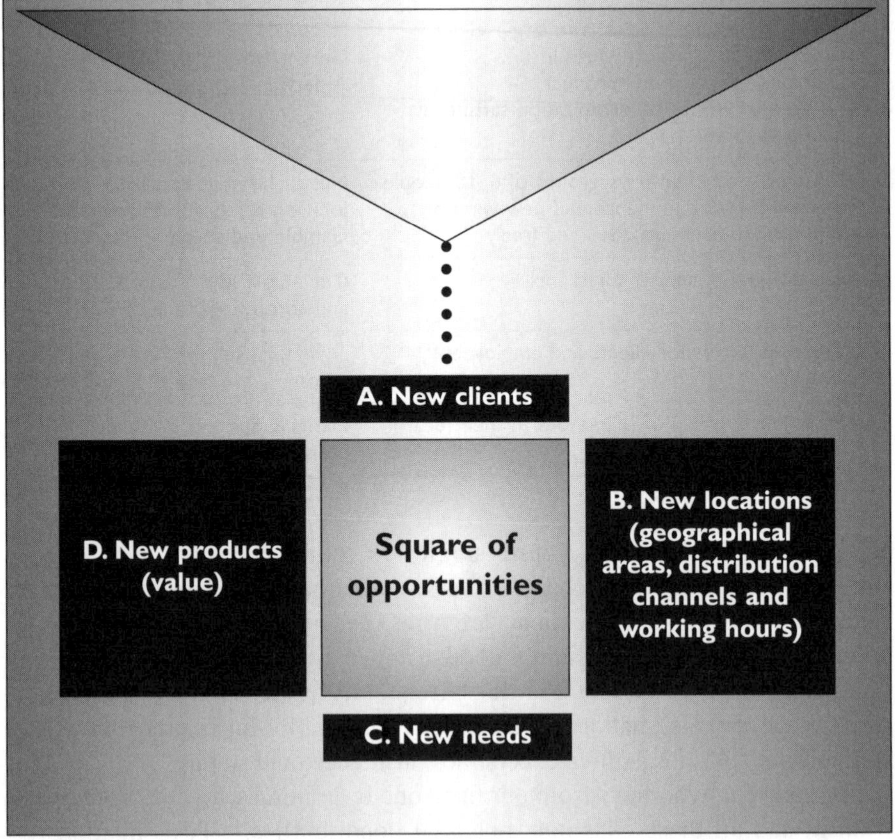

may then occur. Either these opportunities are also suggested by segmentation (because segments are defined in terms of clients); or segments are defined in terms of products or needs and, therefore, the most similar consumers to our present customer base should be used as opportunities.

Let us examine a single example of how the answer to the question 'who is our client?' changed a whole industry, that of the US carpet industry in the late 1950s. At the time, sales were mature in spite of several aggressive marketing campaigns by the industry. Then the industry's association asked itself the fundamental question: who is our client?, who is buying from us?

The data collected was unequivocal: mostly classes A, B and C1 at later stages in life (from full nest to retired persons). This answer gave rise to another question: why aren't younger people buying from us? And the immediate answer was: they lack the money and have other priorities: car loans, mortgages, furniture to buy, the education of their children.

The solution required finding a new type of client who did not have these types of problems and restraints. The industry found it in the real estate contractor, who had several reasons to value a specific product: wall-to-wall carpeting. Indeed, floor covering is one of the few means of cheaply increasing the comfort and appearance of a home, a substitute for the more expensive option of wooden floors. It is therefore profitable for the mass builder to incorporate rugs and carpets in the new homes at the time of building.

In short, the rug and carpet industry achieved success only when it stopped hard selling to its traditional customer base and asked the questions: who *are* our customers and who *should* they be? This developed a new product (wall-to-wall carpeting) to be sold to a new type of client (the real estate contractor).

Client analysis also creates opportunities through three other crucial questions:

- Where is our client? This question led Japanese banks to follow Japanese companies throughout the world and US banks to place ATMs, POS and in some cases small agencies within department stores, shopping malls, super and hypermarkets, airports and train stations.

- Which of our clients' needs are not satisfied at present? The answer led to the birth of cosmetics for women dieting, the transistor, the Walkman, special purpose bank accounts for students and salary advances (early month accounts), special financial products for women, and so on.

- What is value for the client? It should be borne in mind here that it is what the client does with a product that gives it value.

  Xavier Roberts, a US entrepreneur, provides a good example of the last point. Noticing that small girls do not buy dolls but daughters, in order to replicate their mothers' behaviour, he turned his doll stores into 'doll hospitals', where each child is treated to a visit to a delivery room, operating room and nursing room; then she is taught nappy changing and how to treat colds and ear infections; furthermore, every doll has a birth certificate and is the same race and colour as the child. Finally, before leaving the 'hospital' the child is taken to a special room where she makes a solemn oath of 'mother treatment' to the doll she is giving birth to. The consequence of the whole operation was a tripling of sales. Figure 5.1 summarizes how the answer to each question provides four distinct sets of opportunities for a firm.

Let us now turn to how a client analysis system[31] can be used to help our two firms Saab and Caja de Madrid. To simplify, let us concentrate on Saab and assume that nothing much came out of Caja's client analysis. Opportunities for Caja de Madrid will come from the second way of generating opportunities: segmentation (next section in this chapter). Saab's client analysis concluded that of its overcompact car customers, one fifth (0.20) in the US and one fourth (0.25) in Europe would buy a sports car as a second car, provided Saab could offer a model that was competitive in terms of price. The same applies to one fourth of its luxury car customers (both in the USA and Europe). Fifteen per cent and 24% are the real turnover of overcompacts as a percentage of total, in the US and Europe; 5% and 15%, in the US and Europe, for luxury cars. That amounts to:

$$(0.20 \times 0.15) + (0.25 \times 0.24) + (0.25 \times 0.05) + (0.25 \times 0.15) = 0.03 + 0.06 + 0.0125 + 0.0375 = 0.14 = 14\%$$

of its present customer base.

That is, the number of Saab's clients who are interested in a sports model is around 14%. Furthermore, according to client analysis, such clients have five main characteristics: they are relatively young; very active; they try to assert themselves as different; somewhat impulsive; and most of them are males. Thus, they are willing to buy a sports car as long as it is not as expensive as top sports models such as those produced by Porsche, Maserati, Ferrari and Lamborghini. As mentioned in Chapter 3, when segmenting the industry, one usually distinguishes two segments with sports models: cars costing up to $80,000 and top models over that. Saab's sports models fall into the first category (just like most models produced by MG, Lotus, Alfa Romeo and the Mercedes CLK, the BMW 3-series and the Audi TT). This is partly for financial reasons and partly in order not to make the clients feel guilty (after all they are heads of families, supposedly mature men and not buying a toy). In short, these are clients in their late thirties, forties and early fifties who are willing to buy two different types of car for two distinct roles: overcompacts and luxury cars when acting as fathers of medium or large families; and sports cars for weekends with their wives or cruising alone for fun.

The characteristics they look for in the sports car (which will become the key success factors for the new venture) are speed (both in terms of maximum speed and acceleration), competitive price, stylish design and the image of youth associated with it.

We now turn to the other way of generating opportunities: segmentation.

Segmenting to generate opportunities

Segmentation to generate opportunities is based on five steps. First, one must draw the segmentation matrix of all industries the corporation is in. Second, each segmentation matrix should contain the real, actual (and not planned) strategy. In other words, what is important at this stage are the segments where our firm is actually invoicing and by how much, provided they were not eliminated in the evaluation matrix in the previous chapter.

Based on the analysis in the previous chapter, it was decided to abandon no segments for Caja de Madrid and one for Saab: subcompacts for classes B and C1. Since it was decided to phase out operations in this segment, it should be deleted from further analysis. Figures 5.2 and 5.3 present the real strategy for our two case studies of Saab and Caja de Madrid.

Figure 5.2a Saab's strategic plan and real strategy (US)

I

US market Industry: Transport vehicles

Type of Car / **Client**	**Social classes** A	B	C1	C2	D	E	**Organizations** Public/private
Motorbikes							
Subcompacts		Saab 9-1 3%					
Compacts							
Overcompacts	Saab 9-3 sedan 15%						
Station wagons	Saab 9-5 wagon 10%						
Vans (and light trucks)							
Luxury	Saab 9-5 sedan 5%						
Sports							
Mini-buses							
Buses							
Cargo							
Special purpose vehicles (4-wheel drive, armoured)							

Key:

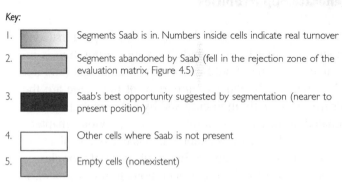

1. Segments Saab is in. Numbers inside cells indicate real turnover
2. Segments abandoned by Saab (fell in the rejection zone of the evaluation matrix, Figure 4.5)
3. Saab's best opportunity suggested by segmentation (nearer to present position)
4. Other cells where Saab is not present
5. Empty cells (nonexistent)

Figure 5.2b Saab's strategic plan and real strategy (EU)

II — EU market Industry: Transport vehicles

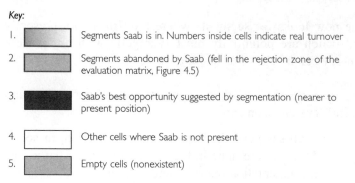

Type of Car \ Client	Social classes A	B	C1	C2	D	E	Organizations Public/private
Motorbikes							
Subcompacts		Saab 9-1 10%					
Compacts							
Overcompacts	Saab 9-3 sedan 23%						
Station wagons	Saab 9-5 wagon 18%						
Vans (and light trucks)							
Luxury	Saab 9-5 sedan 16%						
Sports							
Mini-buses							
Buses							
Cargo							
Special purpose vehicles (4-wheel drive, armoured)							

Key:

1. Segments Saab is in. Numbers inside cells indicate real turnover
2. Segments abandoned by Saab (fell in the rejection zone of the evaluation matrix, Figure 4.5)
3. Saab's best opportunity suggested by segmentation (nearer to present position)
4. Other cells where Saab is not present
5. Empty cells (nonexistent)

Figure 5.3 Caja de Madrid's strategic plan and real strategy

Geographical area: Spain					Activity: Retail banking			
Life cycle / Social class	Young single	Just married	First nest	Full nest	Empty nest	Old single	Retirees	Survivors
A								
B								
C1		5	4	11	8	6	3	1
C2			6	10	8	7	3	1
D			5	9	7	4	1	1
E								

Numbers within the cells indicate real turnover

Key:

- Segments Caja de Madrid is in
- Caja de Madrid's best opportunity suggested by segmentation
- Second-best opportunity suggested by segmentation
- Other market segments

Third, one now looks for segments where the firm is not presently operating and which are potentially most synergetic with our present segments. Synergy can be classified as follows:

1. The *most synergetic of all* are those segments in the same column and line of a firm's present segments.

   There are two such segments in Figure 5.3: just married, in social classes C2 and D. There are none in Figure 5.2 for Saab. That means that, within each segmentation matrix, there is a ranking of segments in terms of synergy, depending on how close, and therefore similar, they are to our present segments.

BOX 5.1

It is possible to quantify the distance (and therefore the potential synergy) between any two segments. Let us take the example of Figure 5.3 which is reproduced below.

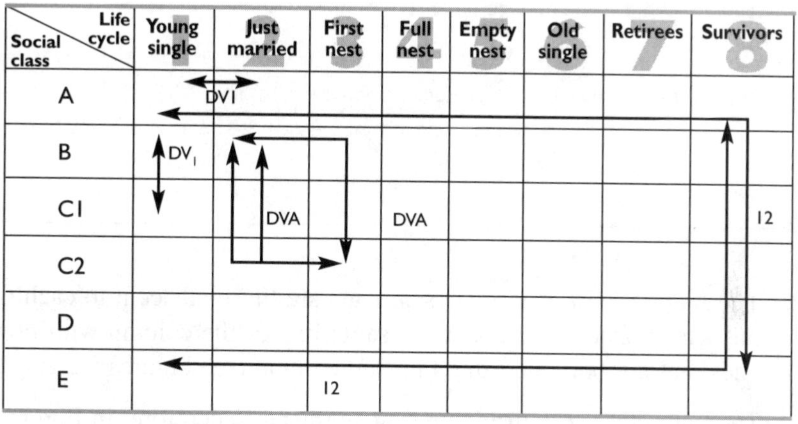

The distance of a segment with itself is zero. The distance between 1A and 2A or 1B and 1C1 is 1, and the distance between 1B and 3C2 is 4 (to reach one segment from the other one must cross 4 boundaries). The maximum distance is between 1A and 8E or 1E and 8A, and is 12 (to reach one segment starting from the other one must cross 12 lines). In any matrix, the maximum distance is equal to (n° lines – 1) + (n° columns – 1).

Since the distance of one segment can be calculated in terms of any other, if one takes the average distance from one segment to all others one obtains the average distance of that segment (regarding all others).

If one then takes the average for all segments, this provides the average distance for the whole strategy (because a firm's strategy is just the segment it is in).

For example, let's assume that a firm is in segments 1A, 1C1 and 3C2. The distance between 1A and 1C1 = 2 and between 1A and 3C2 = 5. Therefore the average distance of 1A is (2 + 5)/2 = 3.5.

Then for segment 1C1, the distance between 1C1 and 1A = 2 and between 1C1 and 3C2 = 3; hence the average is (2 + 3)/2 = 2.5.

BOX 5.1 (cont'd)

Finally, for 3C2 the distance from 1C1 = 3 and from 1A = 5. Therefore the average is (3 + 5)/2 = 4.

Since a firm's strategy is the segments it is in (in our case, 1A, 1C1 and 3C2), one can conclude that the average distance of the firm's strategy is (3.5 + 2.5 + 4)/3 = 10/3 = 3.3.

Given that the maximum distance one could have is (n° lines – 1) + (n° columns – 1) = (6 – 1) + (8 – 1) = 12, the firm has a strategy whose distance is 3.3/12 = 28% of the maximum possible.

2. The *second most synergetic* segments are those adjacent to each other but which share only either the same line or the column with present ones, but not both the same line and column (see Figures 5.2 and 5.3).

   They are close to a firm's present segments. Therefore, in Figure 5.2, compacts, sports cars and vans for classes A and B and overcompacts and station wagons for class C1 are nearer to Saab's present segments.

3. Then there are the white segments in Figures 5.2 and 5.3 whose synergetic potential is lower. Indeed, such synergetic potential decreases the further away they are from the present segments.

Naturally, a firm should consider expanding its operations by the order of the potential synergy of the segments. And it should not consider entry into one segment if there are others with greater synergetic potential. Thus Caja de Madrid should first of all consider entry into segments just married C2 and D (see Box 5.1) and Saab should consider sports cars for classes A and B. The best opportunity for Caja was suggested by segmentation only, and for Saab it was indicated by both segmentation and client analysis.

That means that, in practice, both client analysis and segmenting can be used as tools to suggest strategic alternatives. If one tool indicates nothing (as is the case with client analysis for Caja) one should then use the other. If both point in the same direction (as is the case with segmentation and client analysis suggesting manufacturing sports cars for Saab), that should be the priority.

However, if they point in different directions, in principle, priority should be given to client analysis since its suggestion is based on more detailed information.

Finally, if at the outset client analysis suggests nothing and segmentation indicates several potentially adequate segments, further client analysis, market research and/or management experience should be used to select the strategy with the greatest potential.

Figure 5.4 Client analysis and segmentation working together

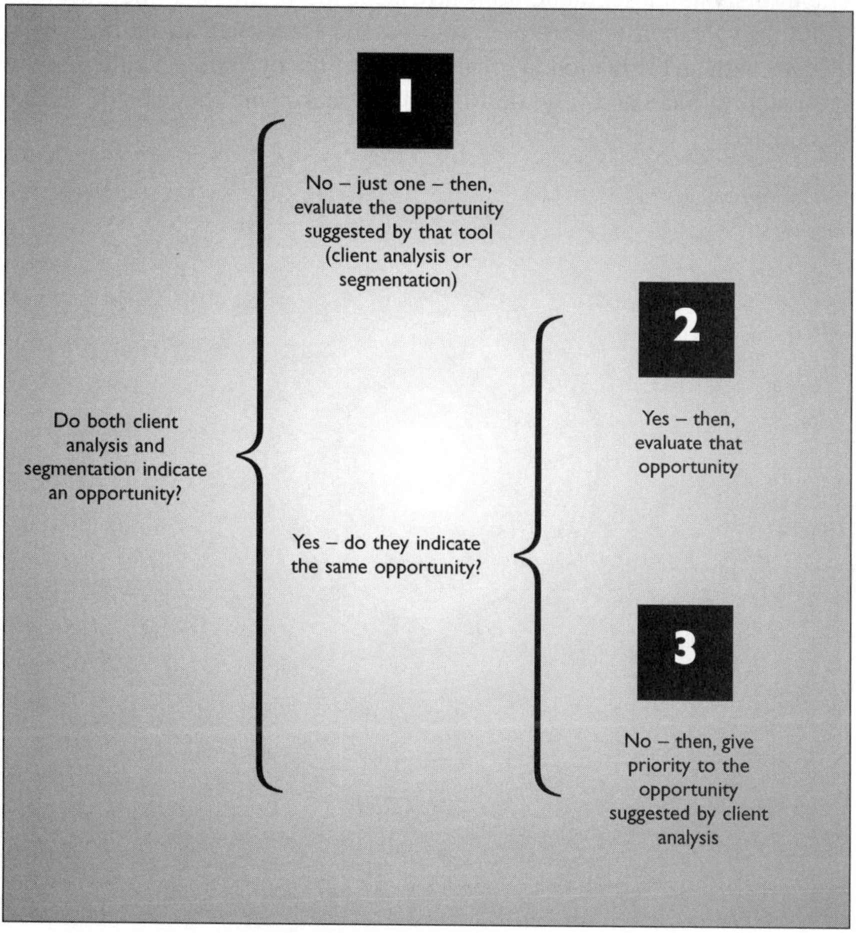

When using both client analysis and segmentation to create opportunities, we have four different possibilities, which are summarized in Figure 5.4 and which show how client analysis and segmentation can suggest strategic alternatives.[32] The use of these methods is straightforward and in practice they provide useful results: very attractive (through client analysis) or synergetic (through segmentation) opportunities.

These opportunities constitute direct market invitations for entry. However, entrances are costly, in time, effort and resources. Thus, before making a final decision, one must carefully evaluate possible strategic movements: in order to ensure they are the right things to do.[33] It is one thing to know the potential of a strategic alternative, be it suggested by client analysis or segmentation, however, the reality may be different. Careful evaluation is therefore required and is covered in the following chapter with an evaluation in greater detail of the two strategic alternatives presented to Saab and Caja de Madrid. To make sure they should indeed be adopted.

CHAPTER 6

Step 4: Evaluating the Strategic Alternatives

In this chapter, the strategic alternatives suggested by Chapter 5's client analysis and segmentation are evaluated.

Figures 6.1 and 6.2 show:

- The present market segments of the previous strategy
- The segments to be abandoned as recommended by the evaluation matrix (Chapters 3 and 4)
- The strategic alternatives suggested in Chapter 5.

The question is: should those opportunities be adopted or not?

The criterion for deciding on any opportunity is synergy, and there are three reasons for this. First, because this criterion was not used in evaluating present strategy; instead, the criteria were attractiveness (rate of market growth, sales volume and sales margin) and competitive position (the degree to which Saab and Caja de Madrid have strengths in the key success factors). Those are the variables in the horizontal and vertical dimensions of the evaluation matrix (Figures 4.5 and 4.6).

Second, it makes sense to select opportunities based on their synergetic potential. Indeed, the greater the synergy, the greater the resource sharing between potential opportunities and present segments, and there-

Figure 6.1a Saab's real strategy (US) (after evaluation by the evaluation matrix)

1

US market Industry: Transport vehicles

Type of Car / Client	Social classes						Organizations
	A	**B**	**C1**	**C2**	**D**	**E**	**Public/private**
Motorbikes							
Subcompacts							
Compacts							
Overcompacts	Saab 9-3 sedan 15%						
Station wagons	Saab 9-5 wagon 10%						
Vans (and light trucks)							
Luxury	Saab 9-5 sedan 5%						
Sports							
Mini-buses							
Buses							
Cargo							
Special purpose vehicles (4-wheel drive, armoured)							

Key:

1. Segments Saab is in which will not be abandoned. Numbers inside cells indicate real turnover
2. Segment to be abandoned by Saab following analysis in Chapter 4 (see Figure 4.5 for the reasons for the abandonment of the subcompact segment)
3. Saab's best opportunity suggested by client analysis (in Chapter 5)
4. Other cells where Saab is not present
5. Empty cells (nonexistent)

Figure 6.1b Saab's real strategy (EU) (after evaluation by the evaluation matrix)

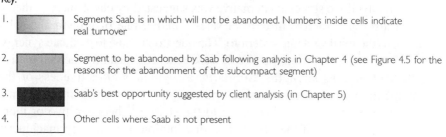

II

EU market Industry: Transport vehicles

Type of Car / Client	Social classes						Organizations
	A	B	C1	C2	D	E	Public/private
Motorbikes							
Subcompacts							
Compacts							
Overcompacts	Saab 9-3 sedan 24%						
Station wagons	Saab 9-5 wagon 18%						
Vans (and light trucks)							
Luxury	Saab 9-5 sedan 15%						
Sports							
Mini-buses							
Buses							
Cargo							
Special purpose vehicles (4-wheel drive, armoured)							

Key:

1. Segments Saab is in which will not be abandoned. Numbers inside cells indicate real turnover
2. Segment to be abandoned by Saab following analysis in Chapter 4 (see Figure 4.5 for the reasons for the abandonment of the subcompact segment)
3. Saab's best opportunity suggested by client analysis (in Chapter 5)
4. Other cells where Saab is not present
5. Empty cells (nonexistent)

Figure 6.2 Caja de Madrid's real strategy
(after evaluation by the evaluation matrix)

Geographical area: Spain					Activity: Retail banking			
Life cycle / **Social class**	**Young single**	**Just married**	**First nest**	**Full nest**	**Empty nest**	**Old single**	**Retirees**	**Survivors**
A								
B								
C1		5	4	11	8	6	3	1
C2			6	10	8	7	3	1
D			5	9	7	4	1	1
E								

Key:

Segments Caja de Madrid is in. Numbers within the cells indicate real turnover

Caja de Madrid's best opportunity suggested by segmentation (in Chapter 5)

Other market segments

fore the higher the probability that a firm will be competitive in the new segments. In other words, there is a positive relation between synergy and competitive position.[34]

Finally, if the strategic alternative was suggested by client analysis then it must also be attractive in term of sales volume, rate of growth and sales margin (the third strategic criterion). The question is how to evaluate synergy.

Synergy comes from the Greek word *synergos* meaning the cumulative effect of various strengths. Similarly, a segment's attractiveness or the competitive position of a company in a segment can be summarized in a single number. This number refers to the sharing[35] between two or more segments in terms of the sales force, distribution fleet, factory machinery, warehousing, suppliers, central departments such as accounting, human resources and so on. Indeed, if the company operated as two distinct autonomous companies, each one working in a different segment, that would require the duplication of all the resources and therefore the costs.

However, these costs will be lower if autonomous companies combine to form two divisions of a larger company instead of remaining separate entities. The lower these costs, the greater the value of the synergy.

Synergy can thus be calculated in an extremely simple way by means of a ratio.[36] In the denominator, one places the whole budget required to operate in a given segment, as if the company division dedicated to that segment was indeed an autonomous entity. That budget is everything which must be spent, a list of all the resources necessary to operate in a given segment of the market and which are part of the business plan, including the number of workers to be hired, the advertising budget, the number and type of machinery necessary, the laboratories to be established, the number of salespeople needed, accountants, office space and so on. All this evaluated in terms of money.

Next, what is saved (by operating as a division of a larger company instead of acting as an autonomous company) is put in the numerator. If a discount of more than 5% is obtained on a quantity of raw materials X, or on parts Y because the suppliers sell a greater volume as they invoice two divisions and not just one, the savings this represents will be recorded. If the sales force of the other division is used, only 60% (for example) of the salespeople will be needed than would otherwise be necessary. This saving is also recorded and so on.

The same occurs for other economized resources: a hypothesis is that the service team costs 70%, the office rent will be 30% lower than otherwise, less security personnel will be required, storage costs will be 50% lower and the use of machines 60%.

The ratio containing the cost savings in the numerator and the total costs (which would be incurred if the company were autonomous) in the denominator gives the synergy. This value can be 20% plus, 15% plus, 5% plus and so on, or negligible if no resource sharing occurs.

Therefore, to evaluate the worth of the alternatives one must calculate all resource sharing between the new segments and all the old ones. This has been done for Saab in Figure 6.3 and for Caja de Madrid in Figure 6.4.

As far as Saab is concerned, let's assume that to enter the sports segment, the company can use the engine of the 9-3 Sedan (overcompact) model with very few transformations. That will save 60% of the engineering development costs which Saab would otherwise incur. If the total life span of the car model is four years, that represents a 15% per year saving in engineering. That is the first value in the numerator of the synergy ratio of Figure 6.3.

Figure 6.3 Synergy of Saab's entry into sports car segment

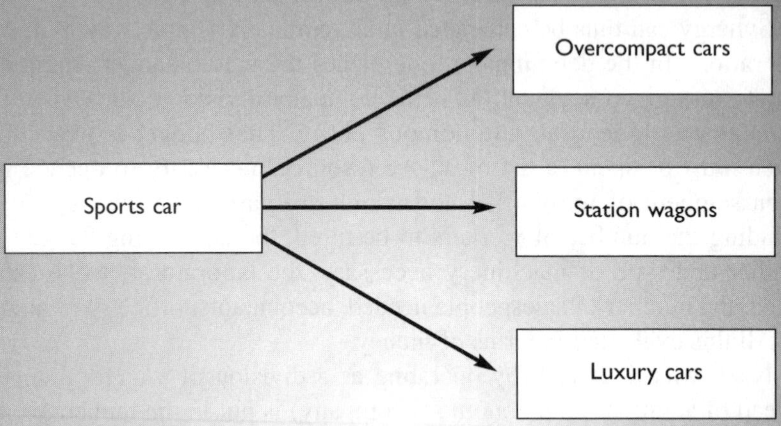

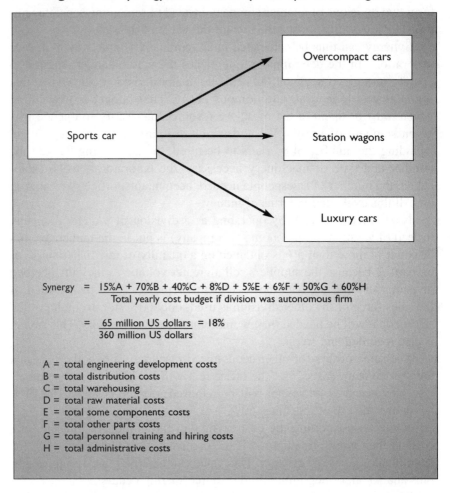

$$\text{Synergy} = \frac{15\%A + 70\%B + 40\%C + 8\%D + 5\%E + 6\%F + 50\%G + 60\%H}{\text{Total yearly cost budget if division was autonomous firm}}$$

$$= \frac{\text{65 million US dollars}}{\text{360 million US dollars}} = 18\%$$

A = total engineering development costs
B = total distribution costs
C = total warehousing
D = total raw material costs
E = total some components costs
F = total other parts costs
G = total personnel training and hiring costs
H = total administrative costs

Let us assume that other savings will occur. In distribution outlets 70%, in warehousing 40%, in larger suppliers' discounts 8% more on all raw materials, 5% more on some components and 6% on other parts. Finally, in the hiring and training of personnel, which will amount to 50% of all costs otherwise incurred. Administrative savings (accounting, human resources department, finance, security and so on) amount to 60% (see Figure 6.3).

Let us assume that no further significant resource savings are possible in other areas such as marketing and production. Then the total savings

Figure 6.4 Synergy of Caja de Madrid's entry into just married C2 and D segments

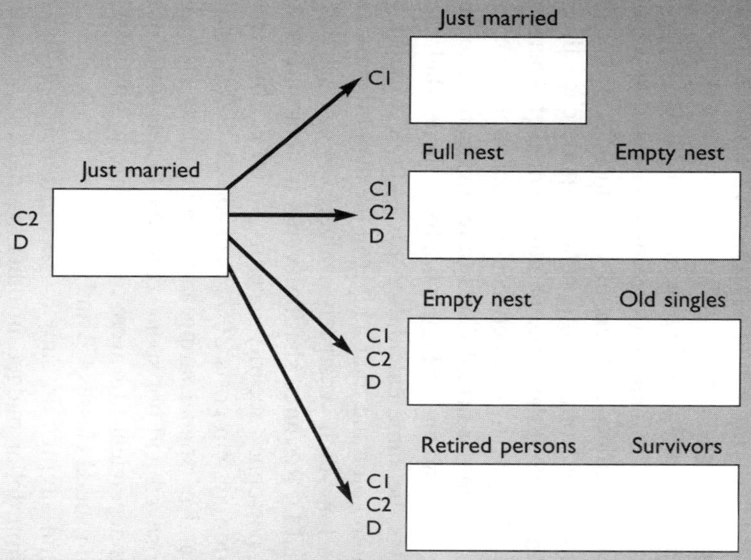

$$\text{Synergy}^* = \frac{\text{60\% central depts costs} + \text{71\% office rent} + \text{30\% info system costs} + \text{40\% back office} + \text{100\% instit advtg} + \text{80\% hiring/training costs}}{\text{Total yearly cost budget if division was autonomous firm}}$$

$$= \frac{\text{80 million dollars}}{\text{123 million dollars}} = 65\%$$

* In this case, the synergy is calculated in terms of what might be saved when incorporating the isolated segment within the company. So it is calculated against all structural costs, not including bank funding costs, which are assumed as relatively proportional, thus with little or no savings.

represent 65 million dollars for a total yearly cost budget of 360 million dollars and the total synergy is equal to 18% (see Figure 6.3).

One should note that synergy in Figure 6.3 is calculated regarding all segments which were to be maintained (overcompacts, station wagons and luxury) and not the discontinued segment of subcompacts. Although some asset transfers could come from subcompacts to sports cars, that would occur at the cost of not selling those assets into the market. Therefore, the simplest way to calculate synergy is between a given strategic alternative and those segments which the firm decided (after evaluation) to maintain (those in Figure 6.1 for Saab and in Figure 6.2 for Caja de Madrid).[37]

Figure 6.4 shows the same calculation for Caja de Madrid. Again, savings are in the numerator and total budget in the denominator.

The market area for which synergy is evaluated is just marrieds from social classes C2 and D. Resource sharing occurs in central departments, such as accounting, personnel, security, catering, of 60%; office space and rent 71%; information system costs 30%; back office 40%; institutional advertising 100%; and personnel hiring and training costs 80%. That is, this money will be saved and not spent, contrary to the situation which would occur if an independent firm were to specialize in this market area of just marrieds from social classes C2 and D.

As a result, total savings amount to 80 million US dollars of an otherwise 123 million dollar budget, in other words, a 65% saving (see Figure 6.4).

Again, with respect to Caja de Madrid, it is important to note that synergy should be calculated regarding all the market areas the firm is presently operating in (independently of whether that was intended or not). Thus, the unintended just married/social class C1 should also be considered (see Figure 6.4).[39] For synergy evaluation purposes, what counts is evaluating resource sharing between potential opportunities and present real presence in the market.

The synergy values in both cases are considerable (18% and 65%) indicating that entry into these new market areas will not represent virgin territory for either Saab or Caja de Madrid. It is only natural that synergy is higher for Caja than Saab, since the former firm moves into an area which shares both the same line and column with present market segments. This is not the case with Saab, where the new area shares only the same column and not the line with present segments. Both companies will be able to transfer to the new venture considerable know-how from previous operations.[38] Furthermore, they will experience lower costs than competition with lower synergy levels.[39]

Finally, 14% of Saab's clients indicated that they will buy the new car (as discussed in the client analysis section of the previous chapter). Five per cent of Caja de Madrid is already in just marrieds, although from social class C1 – see Figure 6.2.

For all these reasons, entrance into the new segments seems advisable for both firms. That would not be the case if synergy were nonexistent or low, for example 5%, 7%, 9%. In that case, the potential opportunities would represent unexplored, virgin territory and caution would therefore be advisable (Box 6.1).

BOX 6.1

In such a case, the entry decision would depend on:

a. The extent to which the strength of the client analysis suggested the opportunities
b. How close those opportunities are to present segments in the segmentation matrix
c. The financial resources available to the firm for the new venture.

The larger the number of affirmative answers to these three questions, the stronger the case for entry. However, if a final entry decision was made, it would be in spite of the low levels of synergy.

In our case, however, the future strategy for Saab will consist of all previous segments, except subcompacts, plus the new sports car segment. That is, the new (future) strategy will differ from the old (present) one, regarding what was abandoned (subcompacts) and adopted (sports cars). And in the case of Caja de Madrid, all present segments will be maintained and the market areas of just marrieds of social classes C2 and D will be added.

Those are the new planned strategies for both firms, their future market stance, their plans regarding what they will and will not do. These plans should be written down and new documents produced. This is dealt with in Chapter 7.

CHAPTER 7

Step 5: The New Strategy

Introduction

This chapter presents the strategic documents which Saab and Caja de Madrid are now able to produce as a consequence of the planning process carried out in the previous chapters. There are two documents:

1. The strategic plan
2. Definition of the mission.

With these documents, the new strategy is defined in very precise terms, that is, on top of the quality of its content, strategy must also have a good format: its precision. Both quality and precision are advantages. The first to achieve effectiveness, the second to attain efficiency (by facilitating strategy implementation). That will bring two advantages:

- First of all, it becomes easier to implement the strategy.[40] The neater a strategy is defined, the easier its implementation.
- Second, in one year from now, when the strategy is reviewed, the first step will be to look at these documents, what their aims were and why. And how reality (real turnover in different market areas) differed from the plan.

So let us now turn to see what these documents look like, based on the analysis of the previous chapters.

Saab's strategic documents

The strategic plan

Figure 7.1 presents the strategic plan of Saab. A strategic plan should always be a very simple and concise document, consisting of no more than five or six pages for most companies and no more than twenty pages for the largest organizations.

For each geographical area in which a firm operates, the plan should contain the segmentation matrix of every industry that the firm is in, together with the segments that the firm wants to be in. In the case of Saab these are: overcompacts, station wagons, luxury and sports cars for social classes A and B (see Figure 7.1). It should be noted that the segmentation matrix should also indicate all other segments in which the firm does not operate, because these constitute future strategic alternatives.

The following pages of the strategic plan justify the option for each segment, one page for each segment. This justification is based on three criteria: attractiveness, competitive position and synergy (see Figure 7.1).

Each segment is described at the top of the page in terms of the product, the need satisfied, the type of client targeted and the geographical area of activity.

For example, the first segment of Saab is:

- Geographical area: USA
- Product/brand/model: overcompact 9-3 sedan
- Need: large family, inner-city transportation
- Client: (mostly) males, social classes A and B

Below the square which defines each segment, the three reasons which led the firm to target this segment are set down: attractiveness, competitive position and synergy. The attractiveness value of each segment in Figure 7.1 is the same as that evaluated by the evaluation matrix (Figure 4.5). As explained then, the process is straightforward. One starts by forecasting next year's sales. This figure is then multiplied by the sales price and the unit margin, producing the total margin for next year.

Next, by applying the forecast rate of growth for the period,[41] the total margin for each of the next five years is obtained. Finally, by summing up and dividing by five, the average yearly total margin is arrived at: 28 000 million US dollars for overcompacts (which corresponds to $28 \times 5 = 140\,000$ million) over the total five-year period used in the evaluation matrix; 25 000 million for station wagons ($25\,000 \times 5$ years = 125 million over five years); 18 000 million for luxury cars ($5 \times 18 = 90\,000$ million); and 23 000 million ($5 \times 23 = 115\,000$ over five years) in the case of the sports model.

That segment's competitive position is then shown on each page. Again, this is simply the figure calculated by the evaluation matrix in Chapter 4: each firm's competitive position is basically its average quality (strength) in terms of the key success factors (for a detailed analysis of how attractiveness and competitive position are calculated please refer to Chapter 4).

In the case of, for example, overcompacts, these success factors are safety, space, reliability and assistance. To calculate the competitive position, Saab and its three main competitors in terms of market share are rated on a 7-point scale according to these variables.

Saab's average ratings in all four success factors, less the average of the three competitors, divided by the latter and multiplied by 100, provides a single value of how much better or worse off the overcompact model of Saab is vis-à-vis the competition. In the case of overcompacts, Saab is 2% above the competition average.

For other Saab models, the competitive position is naturally different (4% for station wagons, 6% for luxury cars and 9% for the sports model). That is a consequence of various factors. First of all, success factors vary (see Figure 7.1). Next, the level of Saab's qualities in them also differs. Finally, the competitors against which Saab is benchmarked also change. Competitors for benchmarks are always those three with the largest market share within each segment. Taken together, these three reasons imply that Saab has different competitive positions, depending upon the car model in question.

Finally, synergy. This was calculated as 18% for the sports model in Figure 6.3. For the other segments (overcompacts, station wagons and luxury), synergy is calculated in the same way and included at the bottom of each page's segment. Synergy must be calculated for all segments since it provides important information regarding the overall ability for Saab to target a given segment. That is, the higher the synergy, the greater the advisability of a given segment. (For a detailed discussion on how synergy is evaluated, see Chapter 6.) The same presentation for attractiveness, competitive position and synergy should be repeated[44] for the European market since the same segments in Europe and the US may differ in sales volume, rate of growth and margin. Saab's competitive position may also be different since competitors and/or key success factors may differ. Strengths may also vary, even if competitors are the same in US and Europe: the image in customers' minds; the strength of the distribution network; the quality of assistance and so on. The same goes for synergy.

Thus, between the US and European market, there are differences in:

1. existing industry segments
2. segments chosen for strategy
3. segment attractiveness
4. competition
5. key success factors
6. strengths
7. synergy.

The strategic plan should contain a separate section for each geographical area. However, since the process and methodology is the same, in order to keep things simple, it will not be repeated in Figure 7.1 for Europe.

In Figure 7.1, the numbers within each cell indicate expected percentage turnover. This number follows last year's real percentage (see Figure 6.1), with the exception of sports cars, which Saab expects will eventually replace that of subcompacts. However, since it is the first year that the sports car has been marketed, a 4% objective seemed more reasonable. Luxury is expected to be at 5%, as was planned last year.

Finally, the segmentation matrix should be carefully drawn up for each geographical area, since, as mentioned in Chapter 2, matrixes may differ from one geographical area to another and, even if they are equal, the segments the firm chooses to be in may differ. Also the industries of choice may vary from one geographical area to another.[45] For these three reasons a segmentation matrix should be presented for each region or country. Saab's strategic plan does not pretend – as mentioned at the beginning of the book – to portray reality but merely to provide an example. Competitive evaluations and so on are merely hypothetical.

Figure 7.1 Saab's strategic plan (USA)

1

US market Industry: Transport vehicles

Type of Car / **Client**	**Social classes**						**Organizations**
	A	**B**	**C1**	**C2**	**D**	**E**	**Public/private**
Motorbikes							
Subcompacts							
Compacts							
Overcompacts	Saab 9-3 sedan 15%						
Station wagons	Saab 9-5 wagon 10%						
Vans (and light trucks)							
Luxury	Saab 9-5 sedan 5%						
Sports	Saab 9-3 coupé 4%						
Mini-buses							
Buses							
Cargo							
Special purpose vehicles (4-wheel drive, armoured)							

Note

In principle, each cell is a segment or niche with somewhat different requirements for success.

Thus the analysis should be made for each cell (one page in the strategic plan for each cell), separating class A and B. However, sometimes cells are not distinct enough to justify a cell-by-cell analysis.

Managers should use their heuristic knowledge and industry experience to combine cells when necessary.

In Saab's case, there is one model for both social classes A and B. For this reason, classes A and B were joined.

continued on next page

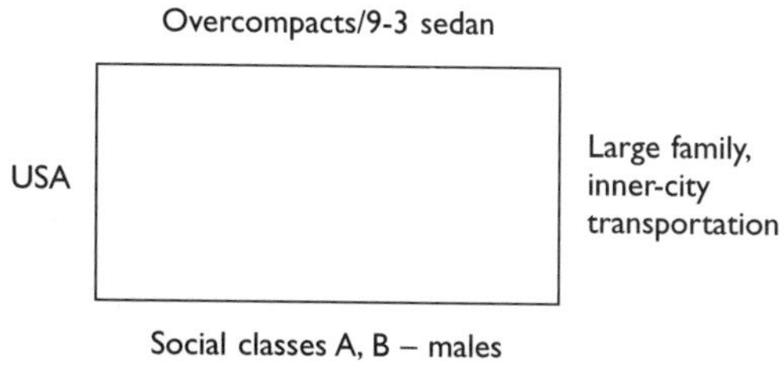

Attractiveness	
A Sales volume (units – cars per year)	4 000 000
B Unit margin	25%
C Rate of growth (next 5 years)	4%
D Average yearly total margin (A × B × C)	28 000 million USD
E Total 5-year margin (D × 5)	140 000 million USD

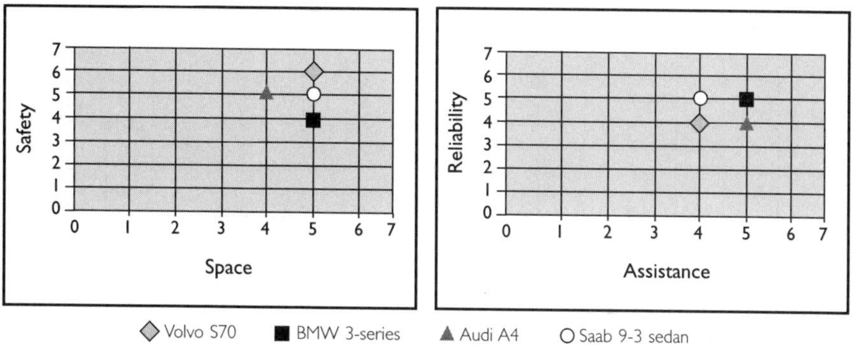

Saab's average [(5 + 5 + 4 + 5)/4] = 4.75

Saab's competition:
◇ Volvo S70 = [(5 + 6 + 4 + 4)/4] = 4.75
■ BMW 3-series = [(5 + 4 + 5 + 5)/4] = 4.75
▲ Audi A4 = [(4 + 5 + 5 + 4)/4] = 4.50

$$\text{Competitive position} = \frac{4.75-\left(\dfrac{4.75+4.75+4.50}{3}\right)}{\left(\dfrac{4.75+4.75+4.50}{3}\right)} = +2\%$$

$$\text{Synergy} = \frac{15\%A + 70\%B + 40\%C + 8\%D + 5\%E + 6\%F + 50\%G + 60\%H}{\text{total yearly cost budget}} = \frac{\text{120 million US dollars}}{\text{790 million US dollars}} = 15.2\%$$

A – engineering development costs
B – distribution costs
C – warehousing costs
D – new material costs
E – components costs
F – parts costs
G – personnel training and hiring costs
H – administrative costs

continued on next page

3

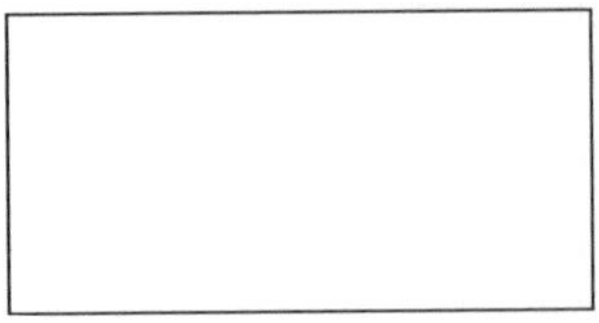

Attractiveness	
A Sales volume (units – cars per year)	2 700 000
B Unit margin	30%
C Rate of growth (next 5 years)	7%
D Average yearly total margin (A × B × C)	25 000 million USD
E Total 5-year margin (D × 5)	125 000 million USD

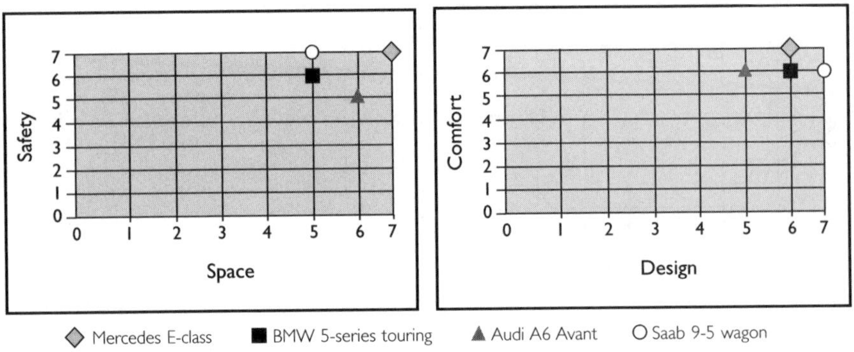

Saab's average [(5 + 7 + 7 + 6)/4] = 6.25

Saab's competition:
- ◆ Mercedes E-class = [(7 + 7 + 6 + 7)/4] = 6.75
- ■ BMW 5-series touring = [(5 + 6 + 6 + 6)/4] = 5.75
- ▲ Audi A6 Avant = [(6 + 5 + 5 + 6)/4] = 5.50

$$\text{Competitive position} = \frac{6.25-\left(\dfrac{6.75+5.75+5.50}{3}\right)}{\left(\dfrac{6.75+5.75+5.50}{3}\right)} = +4\%$$

$$\text{Synergy} = \frac{15\%A + 70\%B + 40\%C + 8\%D + 5\%E + 6\%F + 50\%G + 60\%H}{\text{total yearly cost budget}} = \frac{115 \text{ million US dollars}}{750 \text{ million US dollars}} = 15.3\%$$

A – engineering development costs
B – distribution costs
C – warehousing costs
D – new material costs
E – components costs
F – parts costs
G – personnel training and hiring costs
H – administrative costs

continued on next page

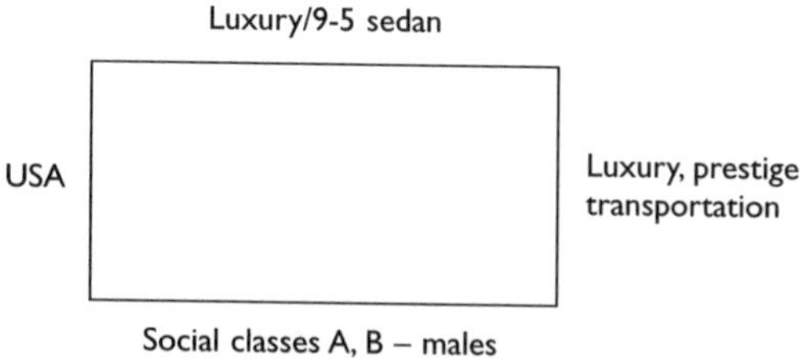

Attractiveness	
A Sales volume (units – cars per year)	900 000
B Unit margin	40%
C Rate of growth (next 5 years)	5%
D Average yearly total margin (A × B × C)	18 000 million USD
E Total 5-year margin (D × 5)	90 000 million USD

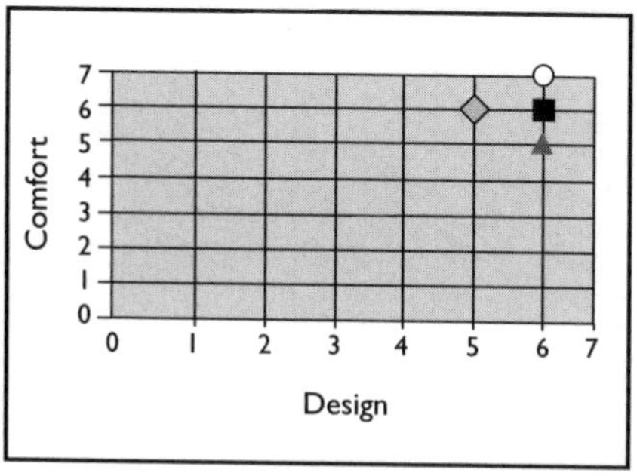

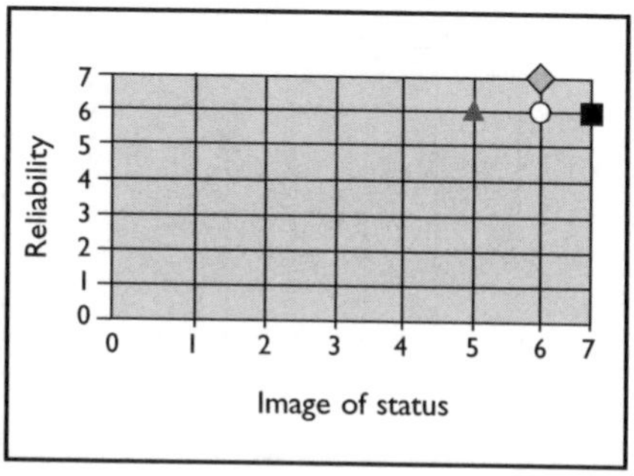

◇ Volvo S80 ■ BMW 5-series ▲ Audi A6 ○ Saab 9-5 sedan

Saab's average [(6 + 7 + 6 + 6)/4] = 6.25

Saab's competition:
◇ Volvo S80 = [(5 + 6 + 6 + 7)/4] = 6.00
■ BMW 5-series = [(6 + 6 + 7 + 6)/4] = 6.25
▲ Audi A6 = [(6 + 5 + 5 + 6)/4] = 5.50

$$\text{Competitive position} = \frac{6.25 - \left(\frac{6 + 6.25 + 5.50}{3}\right)}{\left(\frac{6 + 6.25 + 5.50}{3}\right)} = +6\%$$

$$\text{Synergy} = \frac{15\%A + 70\%B + 40\%C + 8\%D + 5\%E + 6\%F + 50\%G + 60\%H}{\text{total yearly cost budget}} = \frac{\text{100 million US dollars}}{\text{600 million US dollars}} = 16.7\%$$

A – engineering development costs
B – distribution costs
C – warehousing costs
D – new material costs
E – components costs
F – parts costs
G – personnel training and hiring costs
H – administrative costs

continued on next page

5

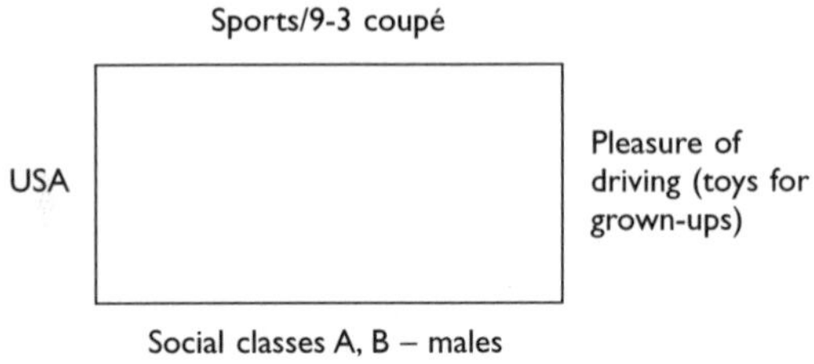

Attractiveness	
A Sales volume (units – cars per year)	1 500 000
B Unit margin	35%
C Rate of growth (next 5 years)	4%
D Average yearly total margin (A × B × C)	23 000 million USD
E Total 5-year margin (D × 5)	115 000 million USD

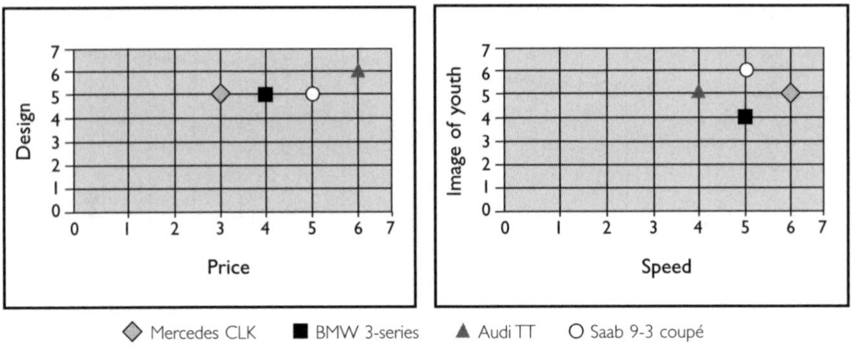

Saab's average [(5 + 5 + 5 + 6)/4] = 5.25

Saab's competition: ◇ Mercedes CLK = [(3 + 5 + 6 + 5)/4] = 4.75
■ BMW 3-series = [(4 + 5 + 5 + 4)/4] = 4.50
▲ Audi TT = [(6 + 6 + 4 + 5)/4] = 5.25

$$\text{Competitive position} = \frac{5.25 - \left(\frac{4.75 + 4.50 + 5.25}{3}\right)}{\left(\frac{4.75 + 4.50 + 5.25}{3}\right)} = +9\%$$

$$\text{Synergy} = \frac{15\%A + 70\%B + 40\%C + 8\%D + 5\%E + 6\%F + 50\%G + 60\%H}{\text{total yearly cost budget}} = \frac{\text{65 million US dollars}}{\text{360 million US dollars}} = 18\%$$

A – engineering development costs
B – distribution costs
C – warehousing costs
D – new material costs
E – components costs
F – parts costs
G – personnel training and hiring costs
H – administrative costs

The mission

It is now possible to define Saab's mission – the business it is in – using the chosen strategy. This is done by composing a short, simple sentence, that captures the essence of the position of the company in the market, its market standing, what it does for a living. The advantage of a mission statement is that, by summarizing strategy and capturing its essence in a single sentence, a focal point will be achieved. This focal point will lead, in turn, to concentration of effort and clarity of objectives within the organization and, by contributing to focus, will facilitate performance.

Since a mission is the definition of the business of a firm, it follows on from strategy, that is, from defining the segments the firm is in. Literature thus speaks of the business mission, the mission of a single SBU dedicated to a specific segment, and the corporate mission which defines the business of the corporation as a whole.

Figure 7.2 shows Saab's business mission document. The first section indicates the various business (SBUs) missions in the USA and Europe. Each is defined by a sentence indicating the product/model, the need it satisfies, the clients and the geographical areas.

It is important to note that the reason for including all four elements in the definition of the mission is so that only the business (the market area) where the company operates will be unmistakably defined. That will provide the precision and detail which Peter F. Drucker argued should be used to define a company's business.

Therefore, there are as many business missions as the number of strategic squares in which the whole corporation operates.

On the corporate level, the mission must be defined solely using the common element(s) of the various squares. If what is common is the client, then this will be used, for example Gerber – babies are our business; if it is the need, for example Johnson & Johnson – toilet products, Yamaha – leisure, Scholl – foot comfort; if it is the product, for example Beneteau – boats, BMW – transportation vehicles and so on.

If among the several business units there is more than one common element (square side), then client, need, product and geographical area should all be used to define the corporate mission. If there is no common element among all the units, then there is no common link between all the firm's operations. In such a case, the whole corporation does not have a single mission, but several sub-missions and, generally, such corporations are called conglomerates.

In Saab's case, the products and social classes are common among all units. The geographical areas, however, are different – US and Europe – and the needs served change between all strategic squares. Therefore, Saab's corporate mission should be defined as a manufacturer of above-average quality cars for social classes A and B in the US and Europe (see Figure 7.2). This is what is common throughout the whole corporation. It thus summarizes Saab's mission. All other aspects (models, male, female drivers, needs) change from business mission to business mission and therefore should not be present in the corporate mission.

Concluding comments on Saab's strategy

The two strategic documents presented in this chapter, the plan and the mission, are based on the analyses carried out in the previous chapters and the sequence of steps indicated.

As a result, Saab now has a very clear idea of what it wants to achieve:

1. To be present in four segments: overcompacts; station wagons; luxury and sports cars, all serving A and B social classes both in the US and European markets (from the strategic plan – see Figure 7.1).
2. To serve the top two social classes in the US and Europe with above-average quality cars (from the mission document – Figure 7.2).

In short, Saab is a top quality car manufacturer, aiming at high specialization, both in the US and Europe.

Figure 7.2 Saab's mission statement

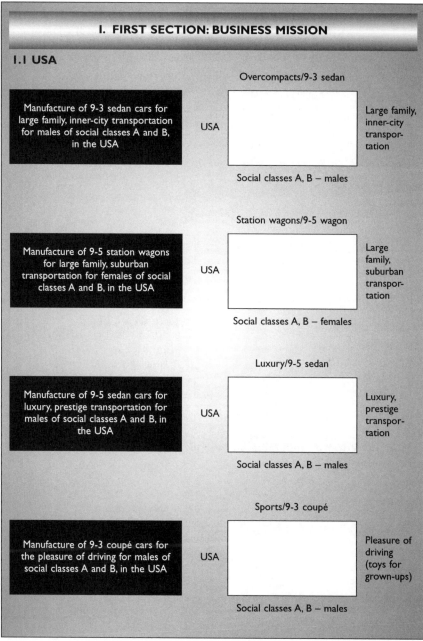

I. FIRST SECTION: BUSINESS MISSION

1.1 USA

Overcompacts/9-3 sedan

Manufacture of 9-3 sedan cars for large family, inner-city transportation for males of social classes A and B, in the USA

USA

Large family, inner-city transportation

Social classes A, B – males

Station wagons/9-5 wagon

Manufacture of 9-5 station wagons for large family, suburban transportation for females of social classes A and B, in the USA

USA

Large family, suburban transportation

Social classes A, B – females

Luxury/9-5 sedan

Manufacture of 9-5 sedan cars for luxury, prestige transportation for males of social classes A and B, in the USA

USA

Luxury, prestige transportation

Social classes A, B – males

Sports/9-3 coupé

Manufacture of 9-3 coupé cars for the pleasure of driving for males of social classes A and B, in the USA

USA

Pleasure of driving (toys for grown-ups)

Social classes A, B – males

continued on next page

Figure 7.2 (cont'd)

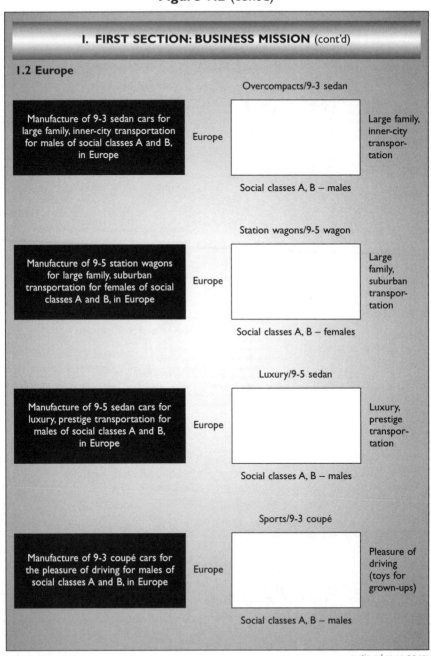

I. FIRST SECTION: BUSINESS MISSION (cont'd)

1.2 Europe

Overcompacts/9-3 sedan

Manufacture of 9-3 sedan cars for large family, inner-city transportation for males of social classes A and B, in Europe

Europe

Large family, inner-city transportation

Social classes A, B – males

Station wagons/9-5 wagon

Manufacture of 9-5 station wagons for large family, suburban transportation for females of social classes A and B, in Europe

Europe

Large family, suburban transportation

Social classes A, B – females

Luxury/9-5 sedan

Manufacture of 9-5 sedan cars for luxury, prestige transportation for males of social classes A and B, in Europe

Europe

Luxury, prestige transportation

Social classes A, B – males

Sports/9-3 coupé

Manufacture of 9-3 coupé cars for the pleasure of driving for males of social classes A and B, in Europe

Europe

Pleasure of driving (toys for grown-ups)

Social classes A, B – males

continued on next page

Figure 7.2 (cont'd)

II. SECOND SECTION: CORPORATE MISSION

To be an above-average quality car manufacturer for social classes A and B in the USA and Europe.

Caja de Madrid's strategic plans

Figures 7.3 and 7.4 present the same documents (strategic plans and mission statement) for Caja de Madrid. Their characteristics are the same as Saab's documents, and they are also a consequence of previous chapters.

Figure 7.3 shows that Caja de Madrid opted for being in a single geographical area (Spain) and solely in retail banking. Within that market it focuses on the social classes C1, C2 and D from just marrieds to retired persons. Social classes A, B, E and young singles are excluded from its strategy. It occupies 21 strategic segments out of a maximum of 48, representing an industry coverage of 44% (21/48). Each cell in the segmentation matrix in Figure 7.3 indicates the targeted turnover as a percentage of total 100%.

Next, the following pages of the strategic plan indicate the attractiveness, evaluation of competitive positions and synergy which led to the option for each segment (see Figure 7.3).

Figure 7.4 shows Caja's mission. The first section details the various business missions and the second section the corporate mission.

There are four business missions, each one relating to a specific area of the market covered by Caja's strategy. These four areas are portrayed in the segmentation matrix (see first page of the strategic plan) and each constitutes a specific market segment, which is then analysed individually in the strategic plan.

In all the business missions, the service (banking), the need (financial services) and the geographical area (Spain) are the same. What distinguishes one mission from the other are their clients, not in terms of social classes, as these are always the same (C1, C2 and D), but in terms of the phases of life cycle that the clients are in.

Thus, in order to define the corporate mission, one must take what is common among all the business units: the service (banking); the need (financial service); the geographical area (Spain); and the social class of the clients (C1, C2 and D). And so, Caja's overall corporate mission should be defined as 'Banking for financial services in Spain for social classes C1, C2 and D, from just married onward'.

Figure 7.3 Caja de Madrid's strategic plan

1 Geographical area: Spain

Social class \ Life cycle	Young single	Just married	First nest	Full nest	Empty nest	Old single	Retirees	Survivors
A								
B								
C1		5	4	10	8	6	3	1
C2		3	6	10	7	7	2	1
D		2	4	8	6	4	2	1
E								

Notes
Note 1 relates to p.1 of the strategic plan and notes 2 and 3 relate to pp. 2-5.

1. In principle, each cell is a segment or niche, with somewhat different success requirements. Ideally, therefore, the analysis should be carried out for each cell (one page in the strategic plan for each cell). Thus in Caja's case, one should ideally separate social classes C1 from C2 and from D and each life stage from another. However, sometimes cells are not distinct enough to justify a cell-by-cell analysis. Then, to simplify, managers can use their heuristic knowledge of the activity to work with different groupings. In the case of Caja de Madrid, four such groupings were considered.
2. In this case, the synergy is calculated in relation to potential savings when incorporating the isolated segment within the company. So it is calculated against all structural costs, not including bank funding costs which are assumed as relatively proportional, thus with little or no registration of savings.
3. Operating margin: the difference between total income (interest plus commission) and total operating costs (funding costs, staff costs, administrative costs, and other overheads).

continued on next page

1. Segment definition

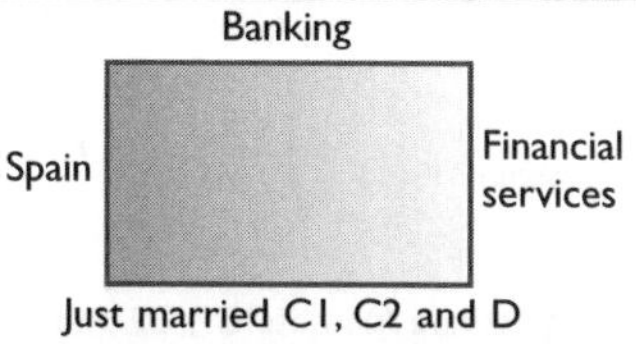

2. Attractiveness (next 5 years)

A Sales volume (total assets)	7 630 million USD
B Operating margin (% on assets)[3]	1.74%
C Rate of growth (yearly)	21%
D Average yearly total margin (A × B × C)	161 million USD
E Total five-year margin (D × 5)	803 million USD

3. Competitive position

	Caja de Madrid	BBA	Santander	Popular Español
Rapidity of service	3	5	4	2
New technologies	5	6	5	4
Image of dynamism	4	5	6	4
Price competitiveness	6	3	3	4

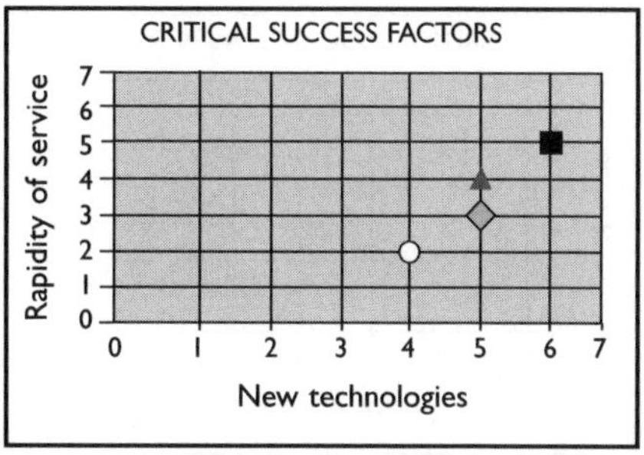

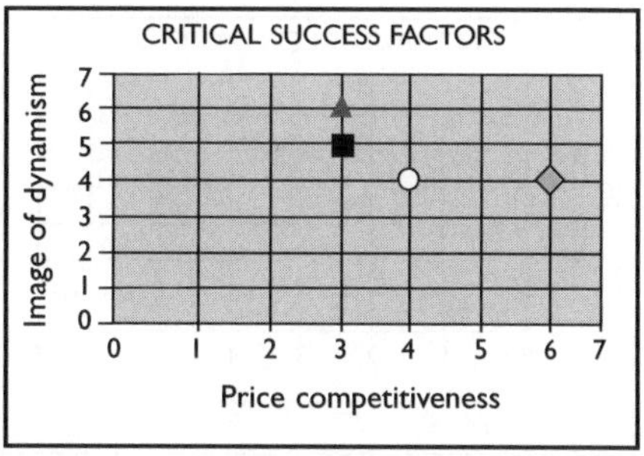

■ BBA ▲ Santander ◇ Caja de Madrid ○ Popular Español

Caja de Madrid av.	4.50
BBA av.	4.75
Santander av.	4.50
Popular Español av.	3.50
Av. of 3 major competitors	4.25

$$\text{Competitive position} = \frac{4.50 - 4.25}{4.25} = 5.88\%$$

4. Synergy[2]

$$= \frac{60\%\ \text{central depts} + 76\%\ \text{office rent} + 30\%\ \text{information system costs} + 40\%\ \text{back office} + 100\%\ \text{institutional advertising} + 70\%\ \text{hiring/training costs}}{\text{Total yearly cost budget if division was autonomous firm}}$$

$$= \frac{\text{USD156 million}}{\text{USD241 million}} = 65\%$$

continued on next page

3

1. Segment definition

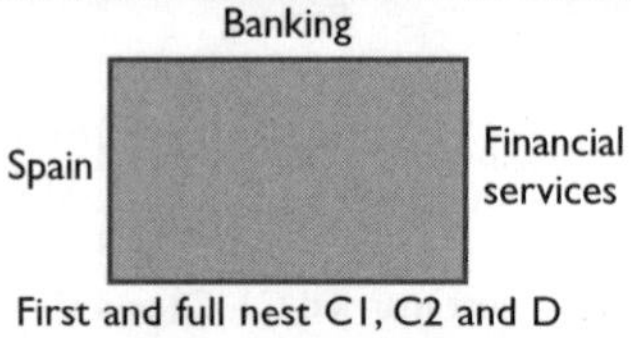

2. Attractiveness (next 5 years)

A Sales volume (total assets)	21 473 million USD
B Operating margin (% on assets)[3]	1.55%
C Rate of growth (yearly)	7.0%
D Average yearly total margin (A × B × C)	356 million USD
E Total five-year margin (D × 5)	1 781 million USD

3. Competitive position

	Caja de Madrid	BBA	Santander	Popular Español
Special purpose products	6	4	5	6
Easy access	6	5	5	5
Image of dynamism	4	5	6	4
Price competitiveness	6	4	5	5

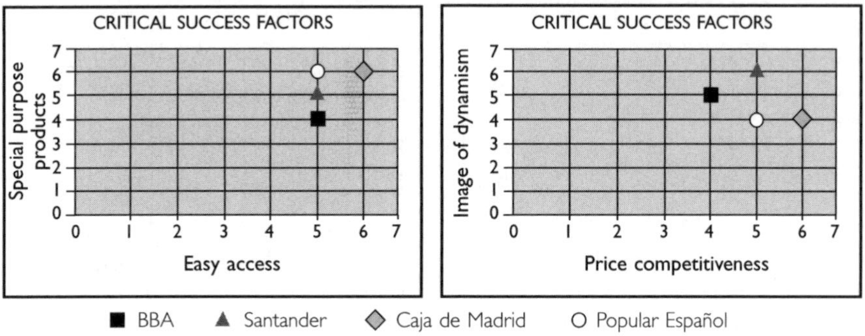

Caja de Madrid av.	5.50
BBA av.	4.50
Santander av.	5.25
Popular Español av.	5.00
Av. of 3 major competitors	4.92

$$\text{Competitive position} = \frac{5.50 - 4.92}{4.92} = 11.86\%$$

4. Synergy[2]

$$= \frac{50\%\text{ central depts} + 60\%\text{ office rent} + 20\%\text{ information system costs} + 30\%\text{ back office} + 100\%\text{ institutional advertising} + 50\%\text{ hiring/training costs}}{\text{Total yearly cost budget if division was autonomous firm}}$$

$$= \frac{\text{USD381 million}}{\text{USD740 million}} = 51\%$$

continued on next page

1. Segment definition

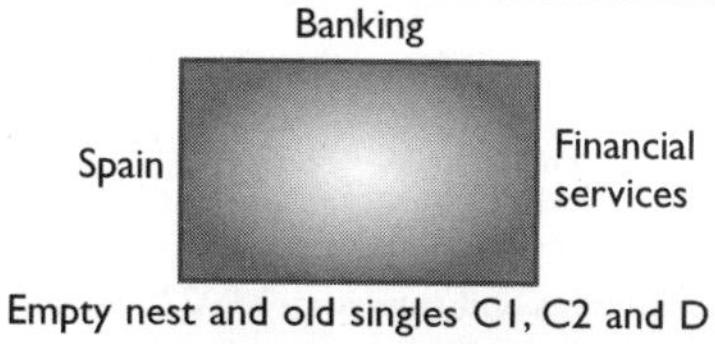

2. Attractiveness (next 5 years)

A Sales volume (total assets)	25 911 million USD
B Operating margin (% on assets)[3]	1.65%
C Rate of growth (yearly)	17.0%
D Average yearly total margin (A × B × C)	500 million USD
E Total five-year margin (D × 5)	2 501 million USD

3. Competitive position

	Caja de Madrid	BBA	Santander	Popular Español
Special purpose products	6	5	4	5
Easy access	5	4	4	4
Personalized service	3	4	4	3
Price competitiveness	4	3	4	5

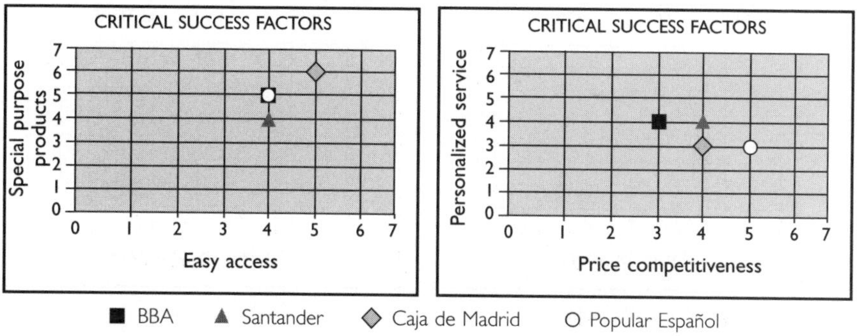

Caja de Madrid av.	4.50
BBA av.	4.00
Santander av.	4.00
Popular Español av.	4.25
Av. of 3 major competitors	4.08

$$\text{Competitive position} = \frac{4.50 - 4.08}{4.08} = 10.20\%$$

4. Synergy[2]

$$= \frac{40\%\ \text{central depts} + 65\%\ \text{office rent} + 20\%\ \text{information system costs} + 25\%\ \text{back office} + 100\%\ \text{institutional advertising} + 40\%\ \text{hiring/training costs}}{\text{Total yearly cost budget if division was autonomous firm}}$$

$$= \frac{\text{USD289 million}}{\text{USD613 million}} = 47\%$$

continued on next page

5

1. Segment definition

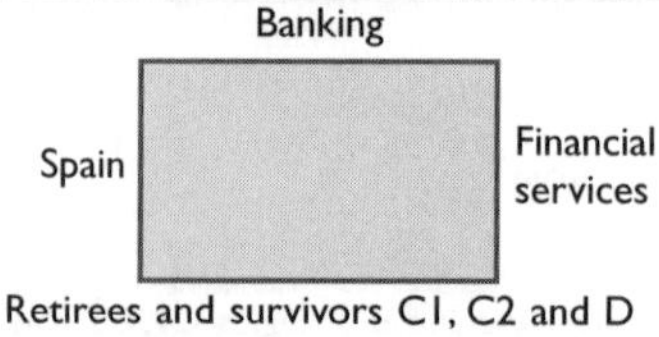

2. Attractiveness (next 5 years)

A Sales volume (total assets)	8 761 million USD
B Operating margin (% on assets)[3]	2.00%
C Rate of growth (yearly)	26.00%
D Average yearly total margin (A × B × C)	221 million USD
E Total five-year margin (D × 5)	1 104 million USD

3. Competitive position

	Caja de Madrid	BBA	Santander	Popular Español
Reliability	5	3	4	5
Image of safety	5	4	4	6
Personalized service	4	3	4	5
Diversity of services	3	5	5	4

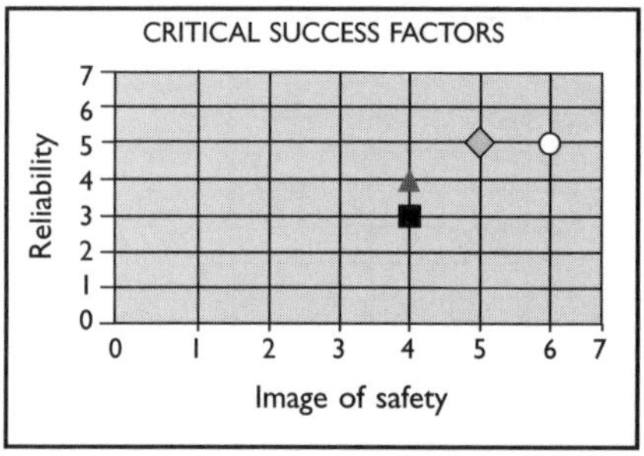

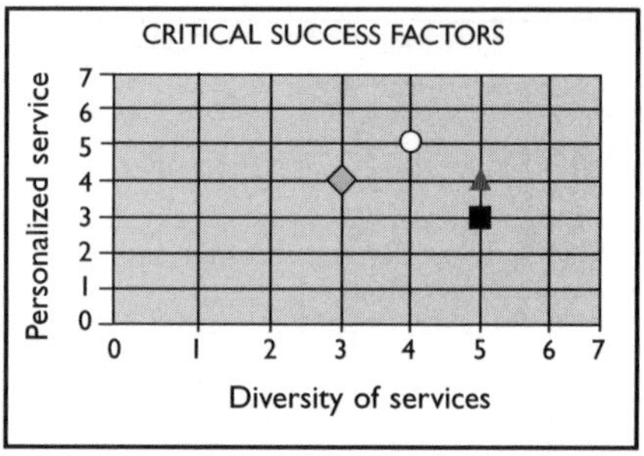

■ BBA ▲ Santander ◇ Caja de Madrid O Popular Español

Caja de Madrid av.	4.25
BBA av.	3.75
Santander av.	4.25
Popular Español av.	5.00
Av. of 3 major competitors	4.33

$$\text{Competitive position} = \frac{4.25 - 4.33}{4.33} = -1.92\%$$

4. Synergy[2]

$$= \frac{50\%\ \text{central depts} + 75\%\ \text{office rent} + 40\%\ \text{information system costs} + 35\%\ \text{back office} + 100\%\ \text{institutional advertising} + 45\%\ \text{hiring/training costs}}{\text{Total yearly cost budget if division was autonomous firm}}$$

$$= \frac{\text{USD124 million}}{\text{USD209 million}} = 59\%$$

Figure 7.4 Caja de Madrid's mission statement

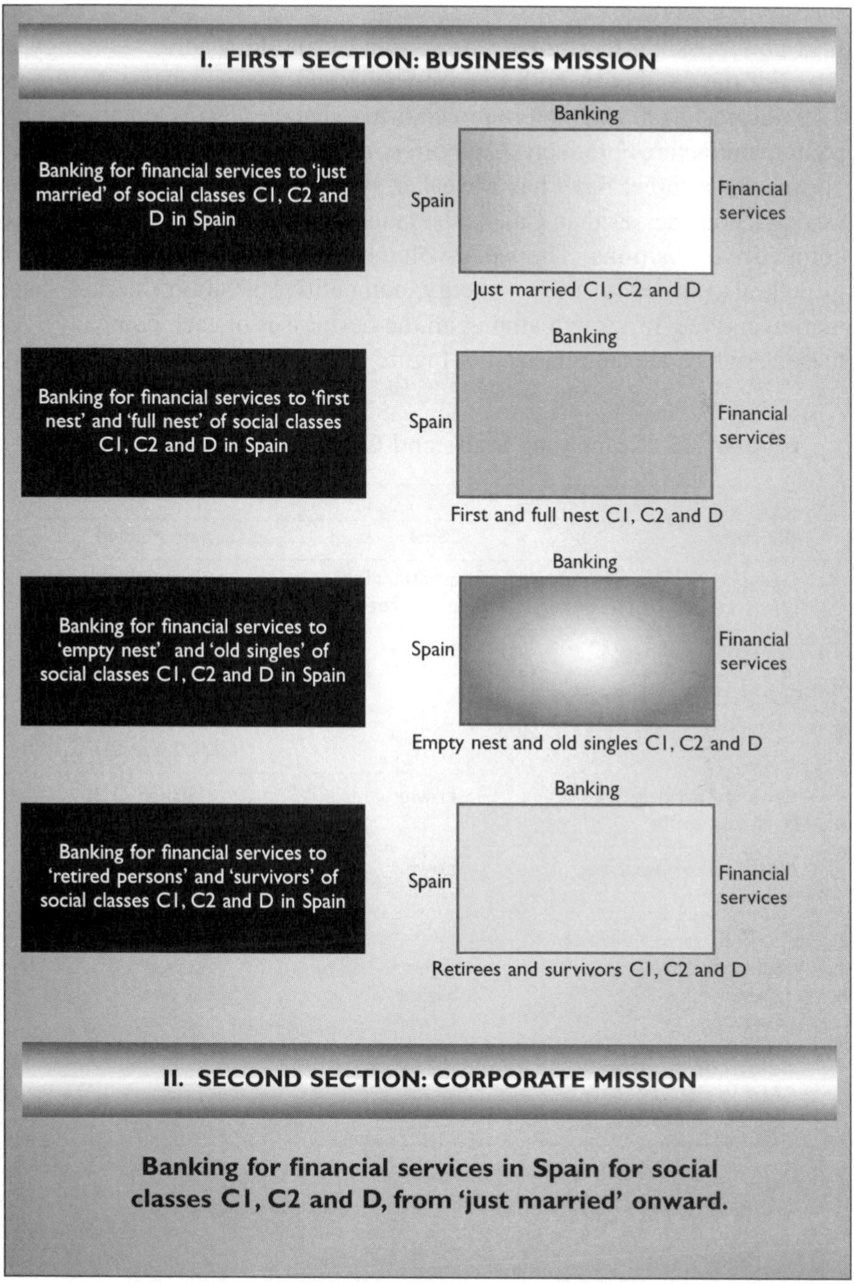

Comparing Saab's and Caja's strategies and missions

It is now possible to compare Saab's and Caja de Madrid's strategy in terms of the content of both their strategic and mission plans. As Figure 7.5 indicates, Saab is an international firm, whereas Caja is a national one; Saab manufactures products, Caja offers a service. Saab serves two social classes, Caja three; Saab has a weaker synergy and competitive position among its businesses than Caja's; the latter enjoys both higher synergy and competitive positions. The sales volume, operating margin and rate of growth also differ (average synergy, competitive position, market sales, margin and rate of growth among all the businesses of each company). All these variables are summarized in Figure 7.5.

Figure 7.5 Comparing Saab's and Caja's strategies and missions

Variables	Saab	Caja de Madrid
Geographical coverage	International (US and Europe)	National (Spain)
Type of business	Product	Service
Social classes served:		
Number	2	3
Type	A, B	C1, C2 and D
Synergy among its business units	Lower	Higher
Market competitive position	Lower	Higher
Market attractiveness:		
Sales volume	Higher[1]	Lower[1]
Margin	Higher	Lower
Growth	Lower	Higher
Major competitors:		
Always the same?	No	Yes
Number in total	4	3

Note

1. Banking volume is usually evaluated by total assets. Sales of a car manufacturer are obtained by multiplying the number of cars sold in the market by its average price.

The basic lesson is that the strategic concepts and planning process developed in this book apply to diverse types of institution, and the best strategy that an organization should follow depends on its own specific characteristics (strengths) and its industry, in terms of rate of growth, sales volume, margins, key success factors, competition and possibilities of synergies. There is no best strategy for all companies but there is definitely a best one for each company, at a given moment in time and with certain available information.

So far, therefore, both Saab and Caja de Madrid have followed the planning steps and as a consequence developed a new strategy. The next step in the planning process has to do with implementing that strategy.

Indeed, after visualizing alternative scenarios,[45] both firms now have a clear idea of where they want to go to. The question is how to get there, which is addressed in the next chapter.

CHAPTER 8

Step 6: Implementation

Having decided where they want to be, Saab and Caja de Madrid must now decide how to get there. That is, after deciding what they wish to achieve, they must now organize themselves to implement that.

It should be noted that implementing a strategy is as important as formulating it. A well-formulated but badly implemented strategy will be effective (do the right things) but not efficient (do things right). The correct execution of a badly formulated strategy will be efficient, but not effective. As the first chapter has indicated, both effectiveness and efficiency are necessary for optimal organizational performance (Figure 1.2).

In order to implement their strategy with maximum efficiency and minimal effort, Saab and Caja de Madrid should take the following steps:[43]

1. Define the structure for the whole corporation, in broad terms, the organization chart.

From that structure derives:

 1.1. How the firm is organized (around products, clients, geographical areas and so on).
 1.2. Where functional departments (marketing, accounting and so on) should be located – centrally or decentralized.
 1.3. The number and location of SBUs.

2. Set objectives (market share, profitability and so on) for each SBU.

Table 8.1 Step-by-step method for implementing a strategy

Step	Question	Criteria
1	1.1 What should be the general structure of the whole corporation?	Diversity/heterogeneity of the several dimensions: products, clients and so forth
	1.2 How many SBUs?	Autonomy of the SBUs
	1.3 Which functions should be centralized/decentralized?	Economies of scale and uniformity versus need for adaptability of the functions of marketing and so on
2	What are the SBUs' objectives?	Critical success factors, market share, profitability and bottlenecks
3	How will objectives be evaluated?	Always in a quantified way and, if possible, objectively (accounting data, secondary data, tests)
4	How will a compensation plan related to objectives be defined?	A percentage weight should be given to every objective and the sum should equal 100%
5	What programmes?	Impact of the programmes on the objectives
6	What structure for the SBUs?	Criticality; similarity; interrelation and the contribution of the programmes
7	How to allocate money (budget)?	In an unegalitarian way

3. Establish how objectives will be evaluated.
4. Define a compensation plan related to objectives.
5. Define programmes (activities) to achieve those objectives: an advertising campaign, a maintenance department, a cost control system and so on.
6. Organize those activities in terms of departments, relating each one with the others, through the organization chart (structure of the SBU – called macrostructure).
7. Develop a budget for all activities within each SBU. When totalled, that will constitute the company's overall budget.

Table 8.1 summarizes this method, step by step.

Let us analyse this approach in some detail and, as always, we will use our examples of Saab and Caja de Madrid to see how to apply these steps one to five. Let us start with Saab.

Saab

The first thing to notice is that Saab's present strategy is based on:

- two geographical areas (US and Europe)
- four products (overcompacts, station wagons, luxury and sports cars
- two client groups (classes A and B).

Step 1.1 is to ask where is the greatest diversity/heterogeneity? Is it among geographical areas, products or clients? Let's assume that diversity (in terms of distribution, legal aspects and so on) is greater among geographical areas and then among the four products. Indeed, all four models in the US and Europe serve only two similar social classes, A and B (and in previous chapters the analysis was made for both together).

So, Saab's overall framework is as Figure 8.1 shows. First the geographical division between the US and Europe and, within these, division first by products and then in terms of functional areas. Since, for simplification purposes, it is assumed that the models sold and the key success factors in both the US and Europe are the same, the structure of the US and Europe are equal. Otherwise, with different car models and success factors they would be different.

Step 1.2 is to locate the functional departments: higher or lower in the organizational chart. Economies of scale and uniformity indicate centralization (higher level in the organization chart); the need for adaptation to various products, clients and geographical areas indicates decentralization. In Saab's case, some departments must be totally centralized due to the importance of the scale of economies (production, development) and uniformity (accounting, planning).

Two centralized departments, namely development and production, handle success factors. The other two centralized departments, accounting and planning, do not handle success factors.

For reasons of low economies of scale, low advantages of uniformity and high need for adaptation, there is one totally decentralized department:

Figure 8.1 Saab's structure

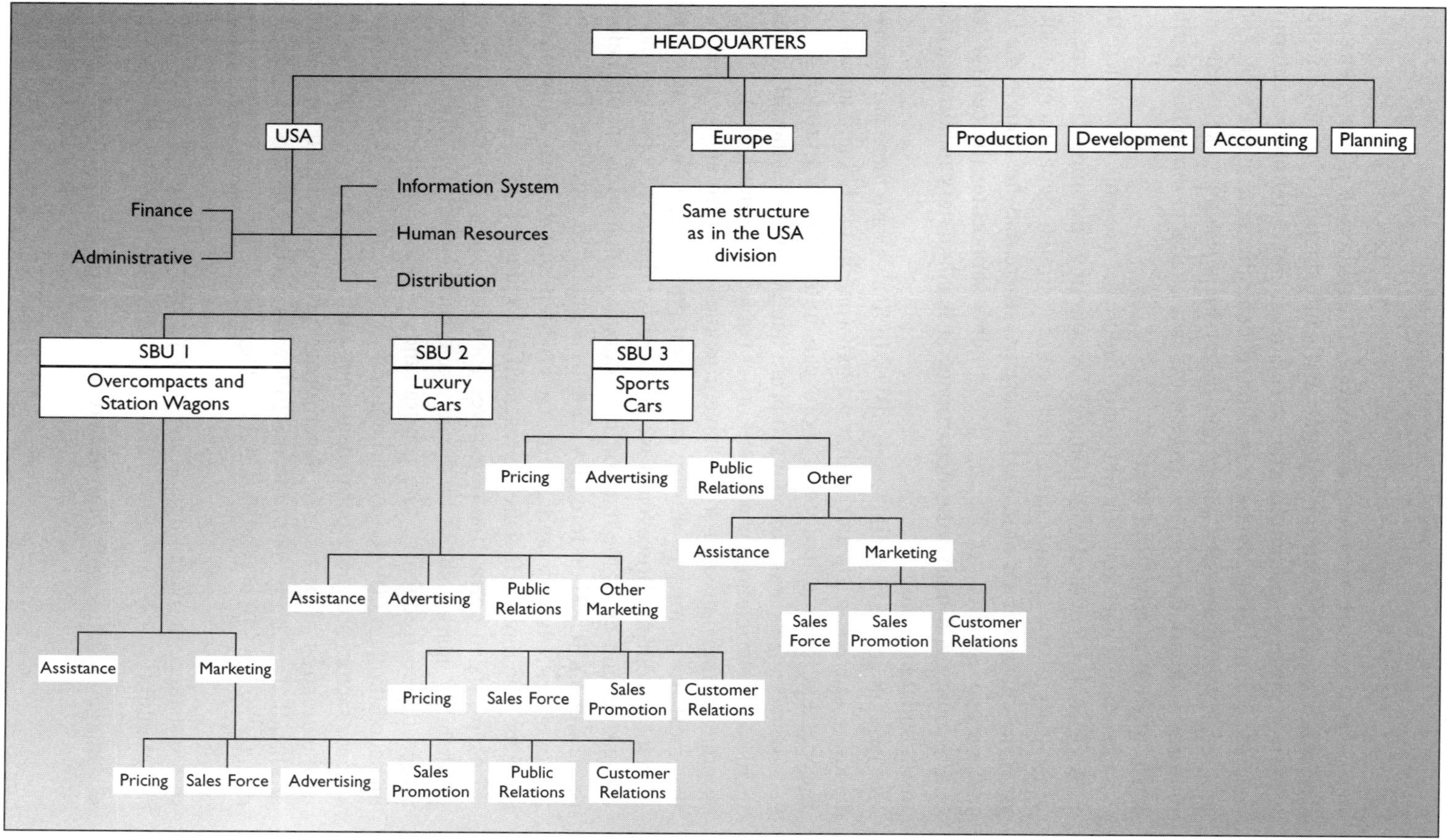

marketing. Indeed, with the exception of distribution all its areas are decentralized. Distribution together with information systems, human resources, finance and administration (management of buildings, catering, security, communications) have medium decentralization, at the geographical level (see Figure 8.1). Above this hierarchical level, gains in scale and uniformity do not compensate for what is lost in adaptation to the specific needs of each geographical area.

One should note that, for simplicity, Figure 8.1 presents only where the bulk of each functional task (finance, accounting, planning) is done. In other parts of the organization, there can be similar departments which perform a narrower set of tasks. For instance, there may be, both in the US and Europe, smaller accounting departments supporting the central one and a centralized marketing department at headquarters handling a few institutional programmes.

Step 1.3 concerns defining the SBUs. In Saab's case there are six: two handling overcompacts and station wagons (one in the US and another in Europe) and four for luxury and sports cars in the US and Europe.

Overcompacts and station wagons are handled by the same SBU, since there is an interrelation or mutual impact between the marketing: changes in prices, campaigns and so on have a mutual effect (in spite of the fact that most overcompacts are driven by men and most station wagons are driven by women). However, if we hypothesise that price, changes and so on make clients cross the lines of the products, both models should belong to the same SBU. Therefore they should be managed together. That is not the case with luxury and sports cars which serve more autonomous markets. The three SBUs are represented in Figure 8.1.[44]

Step 2 is to define the objectives for each SBU. The objectives are profitability, market share, bottlenecks and success factors. Since the first three change frequently, the programmes which implement them are managed through task forces and not framework changes. However, since success factors are more permanent, they justify framework changes, that is, the creation of permanent departments/sections. Some success factors are handled centrally and only the following success factors are handled directly by the SBUs (see Figure 8.2). They are:

- Assistance in overcompacts and luxury cars because of its influence on reliability.
- Image of status and youth in luxury and sports models, respectively.

Figure 8.2 Saab: segments' key success factors

Segments / Success Factors	Discontinued (Chapter 4)	Maintained (Chapter 4)			Adopted (Chapters 5 and 6)
	Subcompacts	Overcompacts	Station wagons	Luxury cars	Sports cars
Price	✓				✓
Consumption	✓				
Manoeuvrability	✓				
Design	✓		✓	✓	✓
Space		✓	✓		
Safety		✓	✓		
Assistance		✓			
Reliability		✓		✓	
Comfort			✓	✓	
Image of status				✓	
Speed					✓
Image of youth					✓

Notes:

1. These are the same success factors as presented in Figure 7.1 (pages two to six of Saab's strategy plan)
2. Naturally, the discontinued segment (subcompacts) does not influence the framework. It is included here solely for comparison purposes with other segments' success factors.

- Pricing in sports cars. The pricing of Saab's sports model is similar to that of an Audi TT, Mercedes CLK and BMW 3-Series, and below Porsche, Ferrari and so on, so that the cars are more price accessible and do not generate feelings of guilt in clients who think they may be buying an expensive toy.

Hence, in the overcompact and station wagon SBU, the department handling assistance must report directly to the SBU president. All others can be decentralized beneath a vice president for marketing. Alternatively, to decrease his control span, one or two marketing functions could report directly to the SBU president. But that is optional. However, assistance is a success factor and that department must always report to him directly.

Within the luxury cars SBU, design and comfort are success factors managed, for reasons of scale (see Figure 8.3), by the development and production departments. These departments also influence a third success factor, reliability, which, however, depends on assistance. Since assistance is a success factor and is decentralized in the SBUs it must report directly to the luxury car SBU president (see Figure 8.3). Then there is the fourth success factor, image of status, which is created by advertising and public relations whose departments, in consequence, must report directly to that SBU manager, too. The other departments can be decentralized further down the hierarchy.

Finally, the sports car SBU has four success factors (see Figures 8.1 and 8.2), of which design and speed are handled centrally by production and development, and price and image of youth (a function of advertising and public relations) report directly to the SBU manager (Figure 8.3). Since sales promotion includes promotional activities, such as discounts on repeat purchases, the purchase of a second Saab car and so on, which impact on price and this is a success factor, the sales promotion department also reports directly to the SBU manager (see Figure 8.1).

So far we have defined:

1. the overall Saab framework (which is organized in terms of geographical areas and then products)
2. the location of the functional departments
3. the number and location of SBUs
4. the departments within it
5. the organization chart of the SBUs.

Now we must define the objectives that each SBU should pursue. These objectives are presented in Figure 8.3, where, for each SBU, a certain hypothetical return (total year margin before fixed costs) and market share level are defined as targets.

Bottlenecks are departments which, although not handling critical tasks, are below minimum/satisfactory levels of performance. To illustrate, it is assumed that, in the overcompacts and station wagons SBU, such a bottleneck exists in the sales department and therefore two new salesmen, with the necessary qualifications and within the budget, must be hired.

Also in Figure 8.3, it is assumed that the luxury cars SBU has no bottlenecks but in sports cars, assistance, although not a success factor, recently has been receiving a large number of serious complaints on the part of customers. Therefore, next year's objective is to bring the level of complaints down by, for example, 30%.

The next step in implementing strategy is to define how key success factor's objectives will be measured. Reliability will be measured by the number of malfunction complaints filed by customers, divided by the number of cars in circulation. Therefore it is a percentage, which is fixed at 2% for overcompacts and station wagons and 1% for luxury vehicles (see Figure 8.3).

Quality of assistance is also measured by customer complaints regarding price, quality, rapidity or personal attendance. The target is to decrease last year's number by 5%. Other targets will also be objectively evaluated: space in overcompacts and station wagons (maintain the former and increase the latter to 50 litres of trunk space); safety in overcompacts and station wagons (decrease stopping time by 5%); speed in sports cars (increase maximum speed from 230 to 250 kms/hour and decrease the acceleration time up to 100km from 8.5 seconds to less than 8 seconds).

The remaining objectives will be subjectively evaluated. In order to evaluate the image of status and youth, a market research firm will survey clients in order to compare, on a 7-point scale, the quality of the image against the competition. The objective is to maintain the 6 and 5.5 image ratings in luxury and sports cars, respectively. Also the clients' perception of price regarding direct competitors should be maintained at the 5 level. One could also use as a yardstick the stripped down, no frills price of our model compared to the competition. However, yardsticks based on client surveys take into account the influence of sales promotion campaigns which influence the perception, but not necessarily always the reality, of compared prices. On the same 7-point scale, comfort and design must both reach 5.5 in overcompacts and station wagons and 6 in luxury cars, and in sports cars, design must attain 6.

Figure 8.3 presents the SBU's objectives, as well as their measurements. These are always based on variables such as: accounting, market or production data (for example space in the cars); information collected by the firm from customers (for example design perception); or by an external market research firm (comfort perception); laboratory tests (for speed and safety) and so on.

The next step is to relate reward to levels of performance on the objectives. Here there are three main aspects to take into consideration. First, as always, objectivity is a plus. Quantification, therefore, is a must. Second, for evaluation purposes, the objectives of a SBU manager should include only: profitability (the ultimate SBU goal); market share (given the importance of market power and scale economies in some segments); improving performance in bottleneck departments; and those success factors, which depend on the SBU managers.

Figure 8.3 shows which success factors are handled by departments within the SBU and those which are managed by central departments outside the SBU's influence.

Thus, taking the sports car SBU as an example, its manager should be evaluated by his/her performance on the success factors of pricing and image and not by performance on the success factors of design and speed which are not under his/her control.

So, the objective of the sports car SBU manager should be those two success factors, pricing and image (measured as indicated in Figure 8.3), profitability, market share and bottlenecks in the assistance department.

Third, for a six-month salary bonus, say, one must give a percentage weight to each objective, reflecting both the total number of objectives and its individual importance. The weights must naturally add up to 100%. For example, for the sports car SBU manager, the weights to calculate the six-month salary bonus could be as follows:

Profitability	Market share	Bottleneck (assistance department)	Pricing	Image
30%	20%	15%	15%	20%

The same method of relating objectives to performance should be applied to the managers of the other two SBUs.

Figure 8.3 Objectives and measurement of the SBUs of Saab

Objectives \ SBUs	Overcompacts and station wagons	Luxury cars	Sports cars
Profitability (average year total margin)	Increase to 3013 million USD	Hold 2520 million USD	Achieve 900 million USD
Market share	Increase to 11.2%	Hold 14%	Achieve 4%
Bottlenecks	Hire two new salesmen	None	Bring number of complaints in assistance down by 30%
SUCCESS FACTORS: Managed centrally (not SBU objectives)	1 SPACE – increase station wagon's trunk space by 50 litres and maintain that of overcompacts 2 SAFETY – decrease stopping time by 5% 3 COMFORT – achieve 5.5 in a 7-point scale 4 DESIGN – achieve 5.5 in a 7-point scale of customer satisfaction	1 COMFORT – achieve 6 in a 7-point scale 2 DESIGN – achieve 6 in a 7-point scale	1 SPEED – increase maximum speed from 230 to 250 km/hour and decrease the acceleration time up to 100 km from 8.5 seconds to less than 8[1] 2 DESIGN – achieve 6 in a 7-point scale of customer satisfaction
SUCCESS FACTORS: Managed by the SBUs (thus SBU objectives)	1 RELIABILITY – 2% number of malfunctions 2 ASSISTANCE – decrease last year's number of complaints by 5%	1 RELIABILITY – 1% number of malfunctions 2 IMAGE OF STATUS – maintain rating of 6 in a 7-point scale of customer satisfaction	1 IMAGE OF YOUTH – maintain rating of 5.5 in a 7-point scale of customer satisfaction 2 PRICING – maintain rating of 5 in a 7-point scale

Note:

1 There is a gentleman's agreement among producers that, apart from high-priced sports cars above $80 000, that is the maximum speed limit.

The final step is to elaborate the budget by specifying the budget of each department within an SBU, then a total SBU budget and finally a budget for the whole corporation. Since this material is to be found in any good book on finance, it will not be developed here.

Caja de Madrid

Caja is both specialized in terms of product (banking) and geographical area (Spain). Therefore, most diversity must be found among functional departments (finance, human resources, marketing and so on) and among clients. Let us assume that there is greater diversity among functions and then among clients, therefore, as shown in Figure 8.4, the first two hierarchy levels should be organized in this sequence. The first hierarchical level would contain functional departments with the single exception of the retail banking department which coordinates the core business of the firm. Further down the departmentalization is in terms of clients.

In consequence almost all functional departments are centralized. The exceptions are the agencies, which incorporate the sales and distribution function, and must be under the control of the retail department, since agencies influence the key success factors of rapidity and easy access (location). Risk management is also at this level, since further down the hierarchy losses in scale economies and uniformity advantages are greater than gains in adaptation.

Still further down are located the units handling sales promotion, public relations and administrative matters (installation, maintenance and so on). Advertising, pricing and product management are decentralized.

The number of SBUs (minimum of one, maximum of four) are determined by the location of the key success factors (see Figure 8.5). Any SBU must handle 50% or more of its success factors, so that the SBU manager may be evaluated by his/her performance on the success factors and overall profitability (which depends on the market segment success factors). Figure 8.6 shows those success factors handled by departments beneath the SBU manager and thus within his/her control, and those success factors managed by central departments and thus outside his control.

The department handling the just married clients has two success factors, image – partly a function of advertising – and price. Rapidity of service within the agencies and technology (ATM, POS, in-house banking) are not within that department.

The first nest/full nest department has within it three of the four success factors: image, price and special purpose products. The exception is easy access, which depends on location, and is therefore a function of the agencies and parking facilities.

Figure 8.4 Caja de Madrid's structure

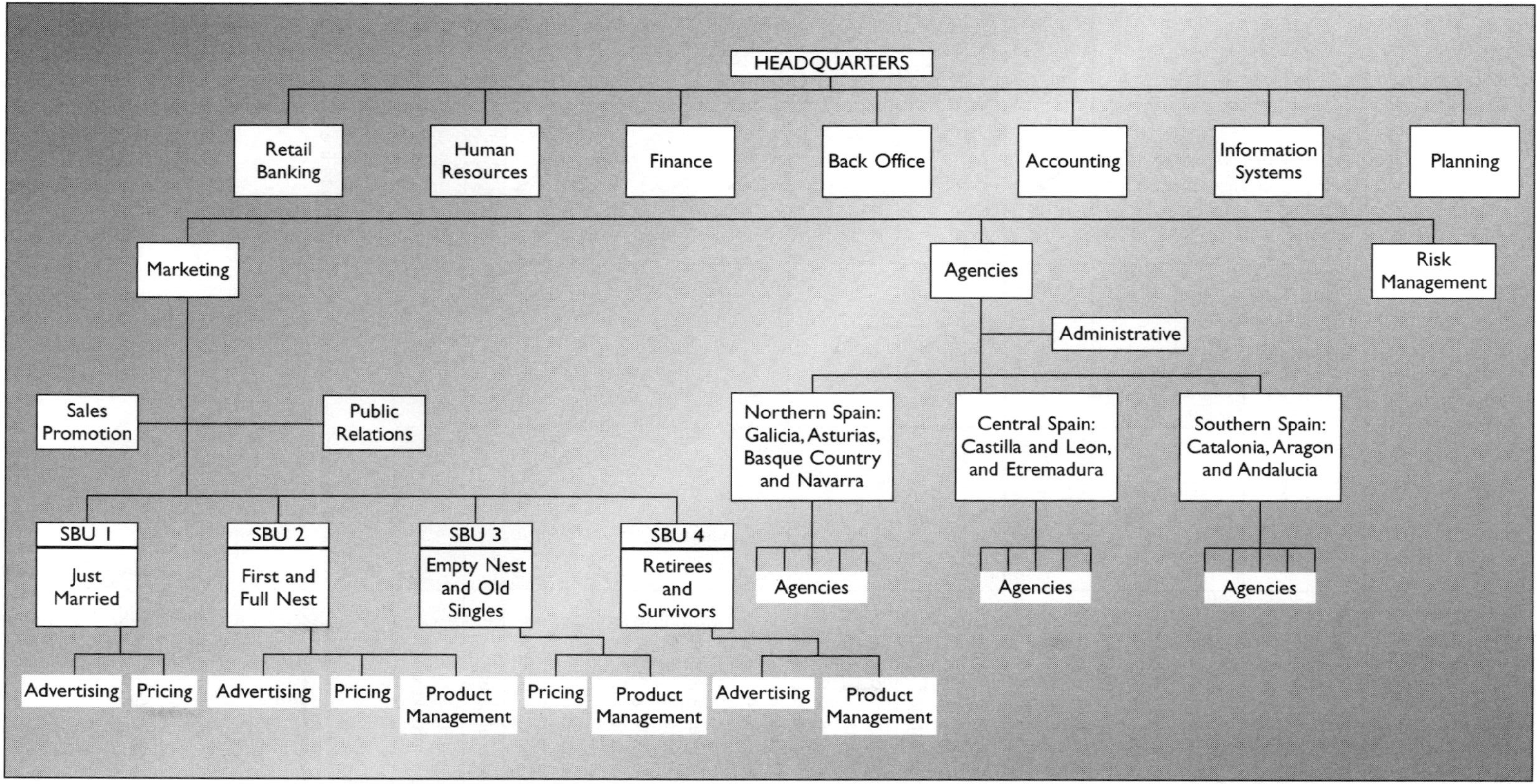

Figure 8.5 Caja de Madrid: segments' key success factors

Key Success Factors[1] / Market segments	Social classes C1, C2 and D			
	Just married	**First nest/ full nest**	**Empty nest/ old singles**	**Retirees/ survivors**
Rapidity of service (within the agencies)	✓			
Easy access through: 1. ATMs, POS, in-house banking	✓			
2. Location, hours of functioning and parking		✓	✓	
Image of dynamism	✓	✓		
Price competitiveness (interest and fees)	✓	✓	✓	
Special purpose products: 1. Home, cars, and so on		✓		
2. University, life insurance, health plans, retirement plans			✓	
3. Home (cleaning, nursing, and so on), travel, medical, and so on				✓
Personalized service			✓	✓
Image of safety				✓
Reliability (few mistakes)				✓

Notes:
1. These are the same success factors as presented in Figure 7.3 (pages two to five of the Caja de Madrid strategic plan).

The empty nest and old singles department controls two success factors, price and special purpose products and does not control the other two, easy access and personalized service.

Finally, the retirees and survivors unit has two success factors: diversity of service (a product-related variable dependant on the existence of special purpose products) and image (partly a function of advertising), and two outside: reliability (few mistakes) which depends on the back office and personalized service (a function of the management of agencies).

In sum, all four client departments control at least 50% of the success factors and in the case of first nest/full nest 75% (see Figure 8.6). Therefore each can be evaluated through a profit or investment budget and considered as an SBU. The SBUs are shown in Figure 8.5. Their objectives and how they will be measured are presented in Figure 8.6.

Again, the principles are those followed in Saab's case. SBUs' objectives must include overall profitability, market share (due to the importance of market power[45] and scale economies,[46] whatever major bottlenecks exist to the functioning of the SBUs) and those success factors which constitute SBU's objectives.

As always, objectives must be measured. Since the bulk of Caja's success factors are not easily evaluated, either by accounting data, external data on tests, one must resort mostly to subjective methods.

The next step is to detail the budget for all departments, SBUs and the whole firm. That will conclude the process of implementing strategy, which was managed by the planning manager.

There is, however, one last task for the planning manager and that is to help each SBU attain its objectives. To explain why and how he/she can do that is the subject of the next chapter.

Figure 8.6 Objectives and measurement of the SBUs of Caja de Madrid

Objectives \ SBUs		Just married	First nest/ full nest	Empty nest/ old singles	Retirees/ survivors
Profitability (average year total operating margin)		1.74%	1.55%	1.65%	2.0%
Market share		Increase from 8.25 to 9.25%	Maintain at 20.2%	Maintain at 32.7%	Maximum decrease acceptable is 2%
Bottlenecks		Hire a new head and a senior assistant for the product development department	None	Replace advertising agency	None
SUCCESS FACTORS	Managed centrally (not SBU objectives)	Rapidity of service – achieve a 6 in a 7-point scale of client satisfaction Easy access – achieve 5 in a 7-point scale of customer satisfaction	Easy access – achieve 5 in a 7-point scale of customer satisfaction	Personalized service – attain a score of 5 in a 7-point scale of customer satisfaction Easy access – achieve 5 in a 7 point-scale of customer satisfaction	Personalized service – attain a score of 5 in a 7-point scale of customer satisfaction Reliability – less than 1% of client complaints
SUCCESS FACTORS	Managed decentrally (SBU objectives)	Price competitiveness – equal to three main competitors in those products representing 50% of turnover Image of dynamism – at least 5% superior to three main competitors as evaluated by client panel	Price competitiveness – equal to three main competitors in those products representing 50% of turnover Products – launch at least two new products which represent at least 5% of total year sales Image of dynamism – at least 5% superior to three main competitors as evaluated by client panel	Price competitiveness – equal to three main competitors in those products representing 50% of turnover Products – launch at least two new products which represent at least 4% of total year sales	Image of safety – equal to three major competitors in those products representing 50% of turnover Products – launch at least two new products which represent at least 3% of total year sales

CHAPTER 9

Step 7: The New Efficiency

Introduction

The previous chapters first defined and then implemented strategy, the former aimed at effectiveness, the second at efficiency. The planning to achieve these two objectives was managed by the planning manager.

The role of the planning department is not restricted to those two aspects. It can have a third role in improving efficiency by helping SBUs to achieve their objectives or, if there is no formal planning, it can help to improve performance in the most problematic departments. Each of these aspects is now discussed.

Role of the planning department in helping to achieve objectives

As seen before, an SBU has different objectives:

1. Profitability (which may require changes in the cost accounting system or in the purchasing department)
2. Market share (new advertising campaign, hiring more salespeople, changes in sales promotion)
3. Key success factors (for example service, distribution channels, modern machinery)
4. Bottlenecks: physical distribution, quality control department and so on.

The planning department can help in these situations for a variety of reasons. First, it has resources and time. If it is properly organized (see next chapter), it will have a small group of people who can be placed in various departments of the organization as necessary to help to implement the objectives: restructuring, warehousing, implementing a client survey and so on.

Second, these people are qualified in areas such as economics, business administration, scientific matters and engineering. Therefore they bring qualified help to problem solving (setting up a new cost accounting system, for example).

A third advantage is that they are one step removed from day-to-day operations where action is needed, which has two consequences.[47]

First, the perceptions of the planning department people will probably be different from those working full time in the operational department. The former will therefore bring a fresh outlook and diversity to problem solving – as the Chinese proverb says: the fish is the last to discover the water.

Second, they bring emotional[48] and political neutrality. These aspects will consequently play a secondary role in shaping the planning department's attitudes and orienting its suggestions.

The fourth advantage that the planning department brings is flexibility.[49] Indeed, planning department staff are a pool of resources which can be applied in the organization as necessary, for example helping to develop new distribution channels this month, improving control of the distribution fleet next, and helping in a client survey after that.

Fifth, although planning department staff may lack the required know-how for the job at hand, they can work under the guidance of external consultants hired to do the job and liaise between the firm and the latter.

Last but not least, they can act as the eyes and ears of the corporation's president, supplying him with first-hand information on the status of the problem and efforts to solve it.

Figure 9.1 summarizes these arguments, indicating the advantages of involving the planning department in attaining the various objectives.

Role of the planning department if there is no planning

It may seem surprising, but even if strategy is not formally defined or implemented as described in Chapters 3 to 8, the planning department can prove very helpful to the president of an organization.

Indeed, throughout the year, regardless of the existence or otherwise of a formal system, two things may happen. First, investment opportunities

Figure 9.1 Role of the planning department

Objectives / Advantages of the planning department		Derived from				
		Planning				Needs arising during the year
		Profitability	Market share	Success factors	Department of bottlenecks	Study opportunities
Time (resources)		✓	✓	✓	✓	✓
Know-how		✓	✓	✓	✓	✓
Distance	Perspective	✓	✓	✓	✓	✓
	Neutrality	✓	✓	✓	✓	✓
Flexibility		✓	✓	✓	✓	✓
Links with outside consultants		✓	✓	✓	✓	✓
Proximity to the firm's president					✓	✓

appear, such as a firm to buy, the possibility of an equity swap, a joint venture for a specific business, entry into a new geographical area and so on.

Then, problems will also arise, such as malfunction in department X, the hypothesis of subcontracting task Y, presently carried out internally by a particular section, or the need to restructure department Z.

Benefiting from its proximity to the president, the planning department can play a fundamental role both in evaluating opportunities and addressing problems (see Figure 9.1). It will bring to problem solving both strength and speed, in solving problems and reporting back directly to the president.[50]

When performing this dual role of analysing opportunities and tackling problems, the planning department will contribute to the structural change of the corporation, both in terms of effectiveness and efficiency, which will help to create the future firm.

In order to play this role, the planning department must have a certain organization, which is looked at in Chapter 10.

CHAPTER 10

Organizing for Planning (The Planning Department)

As seen before, the planning process includes six main steps:

1. *definition* of present strategy
2. *evaluation* of present strategy
3. generation of *alternatives*
4. *selection* of alternatives
5. definition of *new strategy*
6. *implementation.*

Decisions regarding these six steps are taken by line managers. The fundamental role of the planning manager is to supply information for decision making. That information is contained in several documents, namely:

1. document of present strategy (Chapter 3)
2. evaluation matrix
3. document of client analysis (output of the client analysis system)
4. segmentation matrixes (one for each industry)

Figure 10.1 The planning steps and the output of each: the documents

The relationship between — **the documents** / **the planning steps**	**1. Definition of present strategy**	**2. Evaluation of present strategy**	**3. Generation of alternatives**	**4. Selection of alternatives**	**5. Definition of new strategy**	**6. Implementation**
1. Document of the present strategy	✓					
2. Evaluation matrix		✓				
3. Document of client analysis			✓			
4. Industry segmentation matrix			✓			
5. Synergetic potential of the alternatives created by 3 and 4				✓		
6. Strategic plan					✓	
7. Mission plan					✓	
8. Organization chart and SBUs of the whole corporation						✓
9. SBU objectives, their measurements and incentives						✓
10. SBU's programmes and organization charts						✓
11. Overall budget for the company						✓

5. synergetic potential of the new opportunities
6. strategic plan
7. mission plan
8. organization chart and SBUs of the whole corporation
9. SBUs' objectives and how they will be evaluated (and incentives)
10. SBUs' programmes and organization charts
11. overall budget for the company and other control mechanisms.

Figure 10.1 shows the relation between the eleven documents and the six planning steps. To prepare these documents and help to coordinate the meetings at which decisions are taken, three issues should be addressed:

1. How to organize the planning department
2. The personal and professional characteristics of the planning manager
3. The degree of decentralization of the planning department in a large corporation.

Each of these points is now discussed.

How to organize the planning department

The organization chart of the planning department should be as shown in Figure 10.2, comprising three main sections:

1. The administrative section for preparing the planning manual and managing the whole meeting process of inviting participants, preparing the agenda, organizing logistics and so on (discussed in Chapter 2).
2. The information section for producing the information needed for the planning meetings. Some of this information will be collected over the years (client analysis, segmentation matrixes) and other information will be gathered only prior to the planning meetings (synergy between two segments) (discussed in Chapters 3 to 7).

Figure 10.2 The organization chart of the planning department

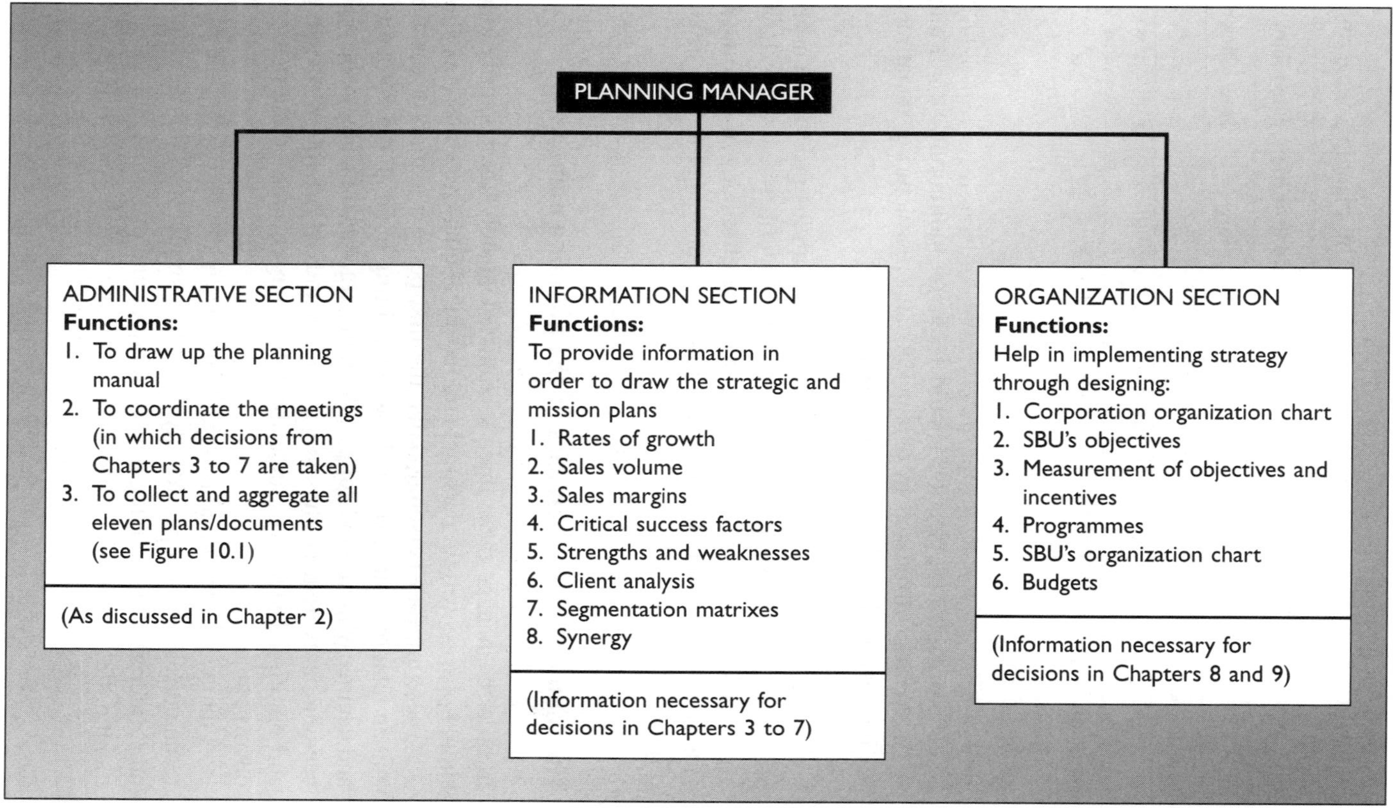

PLANNING MANAGER
ADMINISTRATIVE SECTION
Functions:
1. To draw up the planning manual
2. To coordinate the meetings (in which decisions from Chapters 3 to 7 are taken)
3. To collect and aggregate all eleven plans/documents (see Figure 10.1)
(As discussed in Chapter 2)
INFORMATION SECTION
Functions:
To provide information in order to draw the strategic and mission plans
1. Rates of growth
2. Sales volume
3. Sales margins
4. Critical success factors
5. Strengths and weaknesses
6. Client analysis
7. Segmentation matrixes
8. Synergy
(Information necessary for decisions in Chapters 3 to 7)
ORGANIZATION SECTION
Functions:
Help in implementing strategy through designing:
1. Corporation organization chart
2. SBU's objectives
3. Measurement of objectives and incentives
4. Programmes
5. SBU's organization chart
6. Budgets
(Information necessary for decisions in Chapters 8 and 9)

Figure 10.3 The role of each section within the planning department

Roles / Planning sections	Process	Future firm (time dimension)	
		New effectiveness	New efficiency
Administrative	✓		
Information		✓	
Organization			✓

3. The organization section should focus on monitoring strategy implementation (discussed in Chapter 8) and restructuring departments to improve their efficiency levels (Chapter 9).

The administrative section is concerned with the procedural aspects of planning. The information section covers the effectiveness of the future firm. The organization section deals with the efficiency of the future firm. That is, the last two both contribute towards managing the time dimension (Figure 10.3).

The required characteristics of the planning manager[52,53]

In order to manage these three sections adequately, the planning manager should possess certain personal and technical characteristics.

There are four personal skills, the first being a natural disposition for human relations, since he or she will be sitting in on all planning meetings and dealing with all kinds of people in the organization. He or she will also need empathy, that is, the skill in understanding how other people think, and emotional stability, since the job is largely one of interaction with other people.

Finally, an open mind is needed in order not to eliminate new planning techniques and concepts. Ideally, he or she should be a thinker, a philosopher, interested in studying new techniques and problems and not minding making the decisions and having the prestige which goes with that.

Then there are the technical skills, which cover three areas: technique and concepts needed for the preparation of the strategic and mission plans; techniques and concepts required for organization, and background technical skills.

In turn, these background skills involve four areas: an average knowledge in economics, mostly in the areas of international economics, macroeconomics, microeconomics and industrial economics; some mathematical knowledge (particularly in forecast models); a certain knowledge of the business(es) the organization is in, including technical aspects and production processes; and finally basic knowledge of the functional areas of business administration – marketing, finance, accounting and so on.

Decentralizing the planning department[54]

As an organization becomes larger and more diversified, it becomes useful to have decentralized planning units, as well as a central planning department, in some of the major divisions.

This stems from the fact that in a large, diversified organization the planning system must be basically bottom up and not top down. That is, all the planning processes (and decisions) are taken first at divisional level and then combined at corporate level. Then, a second strategy evaluation is carried out, based on the greater or lower fit among the divisions plans.

Therefore a planning system in a conglomerate would be as follows:

1. The central planning department sends to the divisions a list of the economic sectors which show greater potential growth.
2. The divisions (each including several SBUs) follow the planning cycle as described in this book (Chapters 3 to 8).
3. The divisions send the new strategic and implementation plans to headquarters.
4. The central planning department together with corporate managers scrutinize all documents in search of divisional plans whose rationale is open to question; lower synergy areas among divisional strategies and inadequate divisional objectives. In either case, plans should be rejected or sent back for further explanation.

5. After the interaction between headquarters and the divisions to clarify and solve the issues raised in step four, the final plans for the whole organization would be approved.

In short, the planning process runs as described in the book, but occurs mostly at divisional level (each division is here considered as having one or more SBU). The headquarters' role is first, to supply information on high growth sectors in the overall economy and second, to further evaluate divisional plans (second screening) trying to detect open-ended questions and incompatibilities between the divisional plans.

This means that whatever the organization's degree of diversification, in order to perform its functions adequately the planning department must have the above-mentioned:

1. Organization
2. Personal and technical skills
3. Adequate level of decentralization.

Figure 10.4 Company optimization requires sound management of both the future and present firm

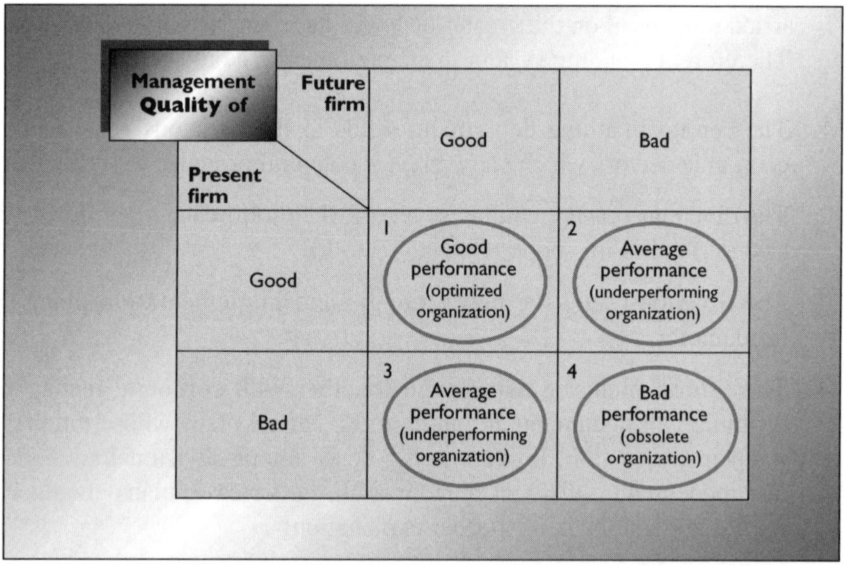

Otherwise the planning process will fail, that is, the planning documents (plans) will not have quality of content. In other words, mistakes in terms of input (process) will create mistakes in terms of output (plans).

In this case, the future firm will not be managed, but neglected.[55] And managers will not be doing their whole job, but only part of it. It will only be a question of time until the whole corporation becomes suboptimized (cells 2 and 3 in Figure 10.4) or even obsolete (cell 4 in Figure 10.4).[56] Time will be working against and not in favour of the organization. And in the words of Joe Lewis: managers will be able to run, never to hide. Sooner or later the future will catch up with them.

CHAPTER 11

Conclusion

This book deals with a firm which is usually neglected and that is the future firm. Neglect comes from two sources. First, a short-sighted view of what management and a manager's role is, leading to a concentration solely on day-to-day tasks and a general disregard for those changes which will create the new, future firm.[57]

Second, even when attempts are made at managing the future firm, this is done, more often than not, in a piecemeal, disorganized way, instead of knowing, from start to finish, the steps to follow, and carefully organizing a planning department to help in the process.

In either case, the result is the same, in that managers perform only half of their jobs, they focus on the present firm, and neglect the other half, the future firm. New ways to achieve efficiency and effectiveness are not properly implemented, if at all, a firm's ability to adapt to its environment decreases, and its competitiveness diminishes. The ultimate consequence is that the risks posed to survival increase.[58] As Charles Darwin so rightly put it: 'it is not the strongest that survive, nor the most intelligent, but the ones most responsive to change'.

And in management the only way to respond to change is through managing the future firm.

Notes

1 That has been a constant since the beginning of business strategy books. See, for example, Ansoff, H.I., *Corporate Strategy*, McGraw-Hill, New York, 1967 and then more recent works: *Strategic Management* by A. Miller and G. Dess, McGraw-Hill, New York, 1996; *Crafting and Implementing Strategy* by A. Thompson and A. Strickland, Irwin, M. Hill, 1998.

2 Mintzberg, H., *The Rise and Fall of Strategic Planning*, The Free Press, New York, 1994.

3 Robert, Michel, *Strategy Pure and Simple II – How Winning Companies Dominate their Competitors*, McGraw-Hill, New York, 1998.

4 Aaker, David, *Strategic Market Management*, John Wiley & Sons, New York, 1994.

5 Christensen, Clayton M., Suárez, Fernando, F. and Utterback, James M., Strategies for Survival in Fast Changing Industries, *Management Science*, **44**(12), Part 2 of 2, December 1998.

6 Goold, Michael, Campbell, Andrew and Alexander, Marcus, *Corporate-Level Strategy – Creating Value in the Multibusiness Company*, John Wiley & Sons, New York, 1994.

7 Mascitelli, Ronald, *The Growth Warriors. Creating Sustainable Global Advantage for America's Technology Industries*, Technology Perspectives, Northridge, 1999.

8 Wind, Sherry Y. and Main, Jeremy, *Driving Change*, Kogan Page, London, 1998.

9 Mahon, John F. and McGowan, Richard A., *Industry as a Player in the Political and Social Arena: Defining the Competitive Environment*, Quorum, Westport, CT, 1996.

10 Vasconcellos e Sá, Jorge, Does your Strategy Pass the No Test, *European Management Journal*, **7**(2) 1989.

11 Brace, Alan and Freedman, Mike, Strategic Planning: Is our Vision any Good?, *Journal of Business Strategy*, March/April 1999.

12 Vasconcellos e Sá, Jorge, *War Lords, Strategy in Dynamic Terms: The Concept of Strategic Reorientation* (Chapter VII) Kogan Page, London/New York, 1998.

13 Robert, Michel, *Strategy Pure and Simple I: How Winning CEOs Outthink their Competition*, McGraw-Hill, New York, 1993.

14 Hofstede, Frenker, Steenkamp, Jan-Benedict E.M. and Wedel, Michel, International Market Segmentation Based on Consumer-Product Relations, *Journal of Marketing Research*, **XXXVI**(February 1999): 1–17.

15 McDonald, M. and Dunbar, E., *Market Segmentation: A Step by Step Approach*, Macmillan – now Palgrave Macmillan, London, 1995.

16 Canals, Jordi, *Competitive Strategies in European Banking*, Clarendon Press, Oxford, 1993.

17 Reynolds, Paul D. and White, Sammis B, with chapters by Nancy Carter and Mary Williams, *The Entrepreneurial Process: Economic Growth, Men, Women and Minorities*, Quorum Books, Westport, CT, 1997.

18 Porter, Michael, *Competitive Strategy*, Free Press, London, 1985.

19 Duus, Henrik J., Strategic Business Market Forecasting, *Strategic Change*, May 1999.

20 Vasconcellos e Sá, Jorge and Hambrick, D., Key Success Factors – Test of a General Theory in the Mature Industrial Sector, *Strategic Management Journal*, Spring 1989.

21 Vasconcellos e Sá, Jorge, The Influence of Technology on Key Success Factors faced by a Manufacturer of Mature Industrial Products, *International Studies of Management and Organization*, December 1987.

22 Vasconcellos e Sá, Jorge, *The Modern Alchemists*, I.E.F.P., 1996.

23 Vasconcellos e Sá, Jorge, A Typology for Industrial Products; Validity and Implications, *Economic Review*, UCP, Spring 1998.

24 Collis, David J. and Montgomery, Cynthia A., Creating Corporate Advantage, *Harvard Business Review*, May/June 1980.

25 Porter, M, *Competitive Advantage*, The Free Press, New York, 1985.

26 Ries, Al, *Focus: The Future of your Company Depends on It*, HarperCollins, 1996.

27 Simpson, Dan, Practical Strategist Questions Count more than Answers, *Journal of Business Strategy*, July/August, 1997.

28 Legare, Thomas L., Strategic Dialogue: Research Process Links Market Intelligence and Strategic Investment, *Marketing Research*, Spring, 1998.

29 Tushman, Michael L., and Anderson, Philip, *Managing Strategic Innovation and Change*, Oxford University Press, New York, 1996.

30 Gibson, Lawrence D., Defining Marketing Problems: Don't Spin your Wheels solving the Wrong Puzzle, *Marketing Research*, Spring, 1998.

31 Trajtenberg, Manuel, *Economic Analysis of Product Innovation: The Case of the CT Scanners*, Harvard University Press, 1999.

32 Hitt, Michael A., Hoskinsson, Robert E. and Kim, Hicheon, International Diversification: Effects on Innovation and Firm Performance in Product Diversified Firms, *Academy of Management Journal*, 1997.

33 Berg, T.L., *Mismarketing: Case History of Marketing Misfires*, Anchor Books, 1991; Walden, G. and Lawler, E., *Marketing Masters*, Harper Business, 1993 or McBurnie, T. and Eluttenbuck, D., *The Marketing Edge*, Penguin, 1988.

34 Vasconcellos e Sá, Jorge, *A Model of the Sources of Benefits in Strategy*, published in the series on Economics and Management, Catholic University, 1990.

35 Vasconcellos e Sá, *A Theory of Synergy, Economical and Social Review*, Lausanne University, 1989.

36 Hitt, Michael A., Hoskinsson, Robert E. and Ireland, R.D., A Mid Range Theory of the Interactive Effects of International and Product Diversification on Innovation and Performance, *Journal of Management*, **20**: 297–326, 1994.

37 Vasconcellos e Sá, Jorge, A Practical Way of Evaluating Synergy, in *Handbook of Business Strategy*, Various authors, *Journal of Business Strategy*, Macmillan – now Palgrave Macmillan, 1989.

38 Rugman, A.M., *International Diversification and the Multinational Enterprise*, Lexington Books, Lexington, MA, 1979; Rugman, A.M., *Inside the Multinationals: The Economics of International Markets*, Croom Helm, London, 1981.

39 McDougall, F.M. and Round, D.K., A Comparison of Diversifying and Non-diversifying Australian Industrial Firms, *Academy of Management Journal*, **27**: 384–98, 1984; Hoskinsson, Robert E. and Hitt, M.A., Antecedents and Performance Outcomes of Diversification: A Review and Critique of Theoretical Perspectives, *Journal of Management*, **16**: 461–509, 1990.

40 Wetlaufer, Suzy, Driving Change – An Interview with Ford's Motor Company's Jacques Nasser, *Harvard Business Review*, March/April 1999.

41 Flywotzky, Adrian J., Morrison David J. and Handelson, Bob, *Profit Zones*, John Wiley & Son, Winchester, 1997.

42 The Big Power of Little Ideas, *Harvard Business Review*, May/June 1964.

43 Vasconcellos e Sá, Jorge, How to Implement the Strategy, Practical Guide for the Little Rabbit, *Business*, April/June, 1990.

44 Champy, J., *Reengineering Management*, HarperCollins, New York, 1995.

45 Ades, Albert F. and Glaeser, Edward L., Evidence on Growth, Increasing Returns and the Extent of the Market, *Quarterly Journal of Economics*, August 1999.

46 Paul, Catherine J.M. and Siegel Donald S., Scale Economies and Industry Agglomeration Externalities: Dynamic Cost Function Approach, *American Economic Review*, 1999.

47 Walton, Sam, *Running a Successful Company: Ten Rules that Worked for Me*, Harper & Row, 1990.

48 Miller, J.E., *The Dilemma of the Corporation Man*, John Wiley & Sons, New York, 1976.

49 Greiner, L., Evolution and Revolution as Organizations Grow, *Harvard Business Review*, May/June, 1998.

50 Johnson, III, E.C., Adventures of a Contrarian in Peter Krass (ed.) *Business Widsom*, John Wiley & Sons, New York, 1997.

51 Hussey, David, Igor Ansoff's Continuing Contribution to Strategic Management, *Strategic Change*, November 1999.

52 Van der Heidjen, Kees, *Scenarios – The Art of Strategic Conversation*, John Wiley & Sons, Winchester, 1996.

53 Vasconcellos e Sá, Jorge, Everything is Important but Some Things are More Important that Others, *Long Range Planning*, Fall 1988.

54 Goold, M; Campbell, A. and Alexander, M., *Corporate Level Strategy*, John Wiley & Sons, New York, 1994.

55 McKelvey, Maureen D., *Evolutionary Innovations: The Business of Biotechnology*, Oxford University Press, Oxford, 1996.

56 Segerstrom, Paul; Anant, T.C.A. and Dinopoulos, Elias, A Schumpeterian Model of the Product Life Cycle, *American Economic Review*, December 1990, **80**(5): 1077–91.

57 Shapira, Zur, *Risk Taking: A Managerial Perspective*, Russel Sage Foundation, New York, 1995.

58 Iygun, Murat F. and Owen, Ann L., *Risk, Entrepreneurship, and Human Capital Accumulation*, American Economic Association, 1998.

59 Schumpeter, Joseph, A., *Capitalism, Socialism and Democracy*, Harper & Row, New York, 1942.

INDEX

T

U

V